Frosty the Snowman

JUST FOR FUN

easy **MANDOLIN TAB EDITION**

CHILDREN'S SONGS FOR MANDOLIN

59 CHILDREN'S CLASSICS
ARRANGED BY DICK SHERIDAN

Produced by
Alfred Music
P.O. Box 10003
Van Nuys, CA 91410-0003
alfred.com

Printed in USA.

ISBN-10: 0-7390-9626-5
ISBN-13: 978-0-7390-9626-0

Cover Photos
Central image models: Katrina Hruschka and Andrew Callahan / Photographer: Brian Immke, www.adeptstudios.com
Mandolin: courtesy of Gibson USA • Moon: courtesy of The Library of Congress • Gramophone: © istockphoto / Faruk Tasdemir
MP3 player: © istockphoto / tpopova • Microphone: © istockphoto / Graffizone • Handstand: © istockphoto / jhorrocks
Jumping woman: © istockphoto / Dan Wilton • Woman and radio: courtesy of The Library of Congress • Sneakers: © istockphoto / ozgurdonmaz
Background: image copyright Elise Gravel, 2009, used under license from Shutterstock.com

♺ **Alfred Cares.** Contents printed on 100% recycled paper.

FOREWORD

This book is designed to be playable by beginning and novice musicians. It's perfect for children, and for parents who want to strum and sing these great songs along with their kids. Plus, matching guitar, ukulele, and banjo books are available— just for fun!

—Aaron Stang, Director Pop and Classroom Guitar
Alfred Music

CONTENTS

A-B-C

TRADITIONAL

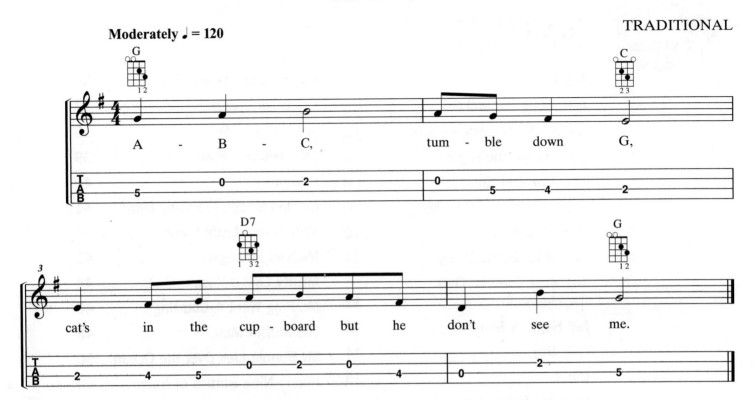

A - B - C, tum - ble down G,

cat's in the cup - board but he don't see me.

A-HUNTING WE WILL GO
(To the Tune of "The Farmer in the Dell")

Easy swing ♩ = 120

TRADITIONAL

1. A-hunt-ing we will go, a-hunt-ing we will go, we'll catch a pig and
2.- 7. See additional lyrics

dance a jig, and then we'll let him go. A-hunt-ing we will go, a-hunt-ing we will

Chorus:

go, Hi! Ho! the mer-ry-o, a-hunt-ing we will go. 2. A-go.

Verse 2:
A-hunting we will go,
A-hunting we will go,
We'll catch a bear and curl his hair,
And then we'll let him go.
(To Chorus:)

Verse 3:
A-hunting we will go,
A-hunting we will go,
We'll catch a deer and pull his ear,
And then we'll let him go.
(To Chorus:)

Verse 4:
A-hunting we will go,
A-hunting we will go,
We'll catch a moose and Mother Goose,
And then we'll let them go.
(To Chorus:)

Verse 5:
A-hunting we will go,
A-hunting we will go,
We'll catch some sheep when they're asleep,
And then we'll let him go.
(To Chorus:)

Verse 6:
A-hunting we will go,
A-hunting we will go,
We'll catch a cow and spotted sow,
And then we'll let him go.
(To Chorus:)

Verse 7:
A-hunting we will go,
A-hunting we will go,
We'll catch a frog behind a log,
And then we'll let him go.
(To Chorus:)

ALL THE PRETTY LITTLE HORSES

TRADITIONAL

ALL THROUGH THE NIGHT

Moderately ♩ = 110

TRADITIONAL

THE ALPHABET SONG

(To the tune of "Twinkle, Twinkle, Little Star")

TRADITIONAL

ANGELS WATCHING OVER ME

TRADITIONAL

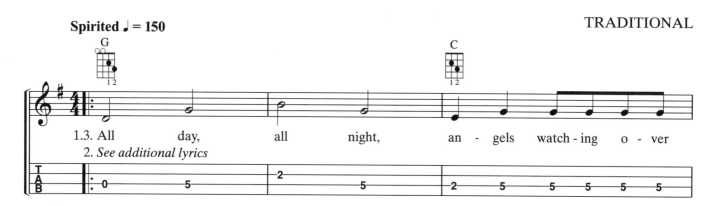

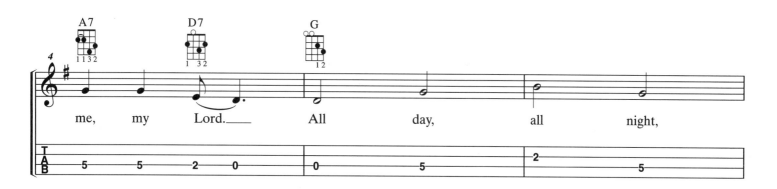

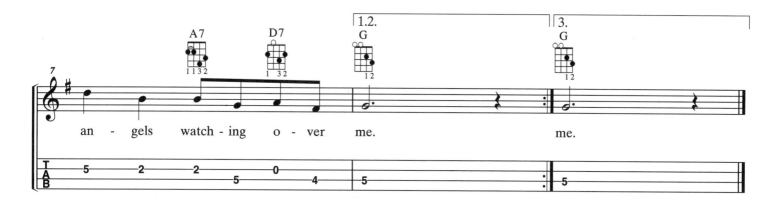

Verse 2:
Sun is setting in the west,
Angels watching over me, my Lord.
Sleep, my child, and take your rest,
Angels watching over me.
(To Verse 3:)

THE ANIMAL FAIR

TRADITIONAL

BAA, BAA, BLACKSHEEP

(To the tune of "Twinkle, Twinkle, Little Star")

TRADITIONAL

Moderately ♩ = 120

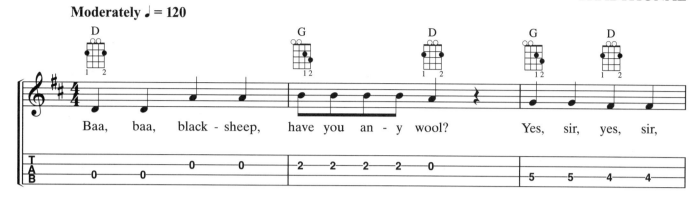

Baa, baa, black - sheep, have you an - y wool? Yes, sir, yes, sir,

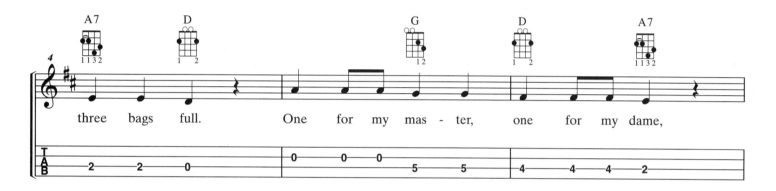

three bags full. One for my mas - ter, one for my dame,

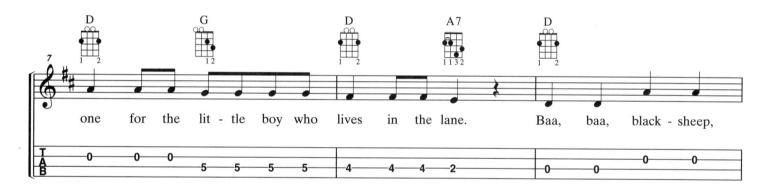

one for the lit - tle boy who lives in the lane. Baa, baa, black - sheep,

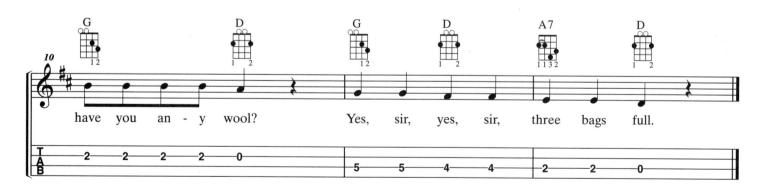

have you an - y wool? Yes, sir, yes, sir, three bags full.

THE BEAR CLIMBED OVER THE MOUNTAIN

(To the tune of "For He's a Jolly Good Fellow")

TRADITIONAL

Moderately fast ♪ = 130

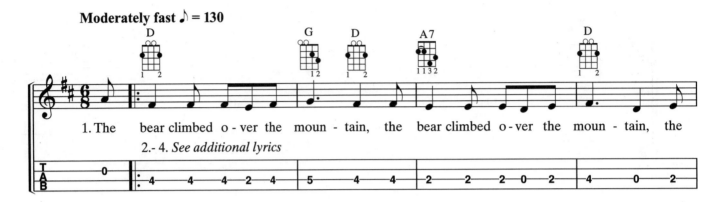

1. The bear climbed o-ver the moun-tain, the bear climbed o-ver the moun-tain, the
2.-4. *See additional lyrics*

bear climbed o-ver the moun-tain to see what he could see.___ 2. He see.___

Verses 2 & 4:
He saw another mountain,
He saw another mountain,
He saw another mountain
And that's what he could see.

Verse 3:
He climbed that other mountain,
He climbed that other mountain,
He climbed that other mountain
To see what he could see.
(To Verse 4:)

BILL HOGAN'S GOAT

TRADITIONAL

Verse 2:
One day that goat
Was feeling fine,
Ate three red shirts
Right off the line.
His master came,
Gave him a whack,
And tied him to
A railroad track.

Verse 3:
The whistle blew,
The train was nigh,
The poor goat knew
That he might die.
He gave three shrieks
Of mortal pain,
Coughed up the shirts
And flagged the train.

BILLY BOY

Moderately ♩ = 120

TRADITIONAL

1. Oh,__ where have you been, Bill - y Boy, Bill - y Boy? Oh,__ where have you been, charm - ing

2. - 4. *See additional lyrics*

Bill - y? I've been out to seek a wife, she's the true love of my life. She's a

young thing and can - not leave her moth - er. 2. Did__ moth - er.

Verse 2:
Did she bid you to come in,
Billy Boy, Billy Boy?
Did she bid you to come in,
Charming Billy?
Yes, she bade me to come in
There's a dimple in her chin,
She's a young thing and cannot leave her mother.

Verse 3:
Can she bake a cherry pie,
Billy Boy, Billy Boy?
Can she bake a cherry pie,
Charming Billy?
She can bake a cherry pie
Quick's a cat can wink its eye,
She's a young thing and cannot leave her mother.

Verse 4:
How old is she,
Billy Boy, Billy Boy?
How old is she,
Charming Billy?
Three times six and four times seven,
Twenty-eight and eleven,
She's a young thing and cannot leave her mother.

BINGO

Moderately fast ♩ = 140

TRADITIONAL

There was a farm - er who had a dog, and Bing - o was his name - o. B I N G O, B I N G O, B I N G O and Bing - o was his name - o.

Each time the song is repeated, successively substitute a clap for one of the letters of Bingo's name. 1st time: CLAP-I-N-G-O; 2nd time: CLAP-CLAP-N-G-O; 3rd time: CLAP-CLAP-CLAP-G-O, etc. Last time: substitute all letters with clapping.

BLUE JAY PULLED
THE FOUR-HORSE PLOW

TRADITIONAL

Verse 2:
Saturday night and Sunday too,
True love on my mind.
Monday morning come around,
And then we'll rise and shine.
(Hum)

BOBBY SHAFTO

Moderately ♩ = 100

TRADITIONAL ENGLISH

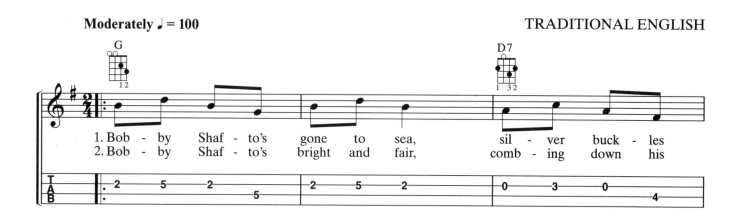

1. Bob - by Shaf - to's gone to sea, sil - ver buck - les
2. Bob - by Shaf - to's bright and fair, comb - ing down his

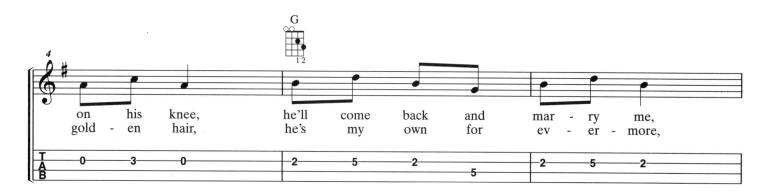

on his knee, he'll come back and mar - ry me,
gold - en hair, he's my own and for ev - er - more,

bon - ny Bob - by Shaf - to. Shaf - to.
bon - ny Bob - by

BRAHMS' LULLABY
(Cradle Song)

By
JOHANNES BRAHMS

Moderately ♩ = 100

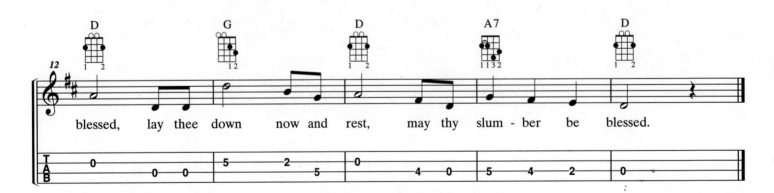

COME LITTLE LEAVES

Words by
GEORGE COOPER

TRADITIONAL
MELODY

Verse 2:
Soon as the leaves heard the wind's loud call,
Down they came fluttering, one and all;
Over the brown fields they danced and flew,
Singing the soft little songs they knew.

Verse 3:
Dancing and twirling the little leaves went,
Winter had called them and they were content;
Soon fast asleep in their earthly beds,
The snow laid a soft mantle over their heads.

DID YOU EVER SEE A LASSIE?

(To the tune of "Ach! Du Lieber, Augustin")

TRADITIONAL

Verse 2:
Did you ever see a laddie,
A laddie, a laddie,
Did you ever see a laddie
Go this way and that?
Go this way and that way,
Go this way and that way.
Did you ever see a laddie
Go this way and that?

Alternate Lyric:
The more we get together,
Together, together,
The more we get together
The happier we'll be.
'Cause your friends are my friends,
And my friends are your friends.
The more we get together
The happier we'll be.

DO YOUR EARS HANG LOW?

Moderately ♩ = 120

TRADITIONAL

Verse 2:
Do your ears flip-flop?
Can you use 'em as a mop?
Are they stringy at the bottom?
Are they curly at the top?
Can you use 'em for a swatter?
Can you use 'em for a blotter?
Do your ears flip-flop?

Verse 3:
Do your ears stick out?
Can you wiggle 'em about?
Can you flap 'em up and down
As you fly around the town?
Can you shut 'em up for sure
When you hear an awful bore?
Do your ears stick out?

Verse 4:
Do your ears stand high?
Do they reach up to the sky?
Do they droop when they are wet?
Do they stiffen when they're dry?
Can you summon o'er your neighbor
With a minimum of labor?
Do your ears stand high?

THE FARMER IN THE DELL

TRADITIONAL

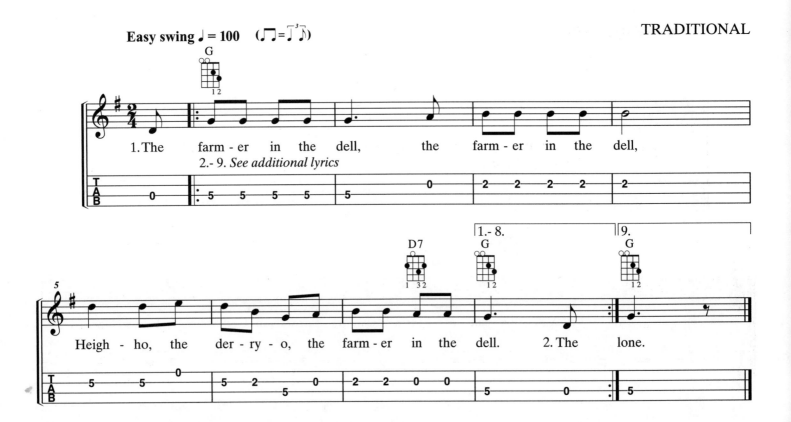

Verse 2:
The farmer takes a wife,
The farmer takes a wife,
Heigh-ho, the derry-o,
The farmer takes a wife.

Verse 3:
The wife takes a child,
The wife takes a child,
Heigh-ho, the derry-o,
The wife takes a child.

Verse 4:
The child takes a nurse,
The child takes a nurse,
Heigh-ho, the derry-o,
The child takes a nurse.

Verse 5:
The nurse takes a dog,
The nurse takes a dog,
Heigh-ho, the derry-o,
The nurse takes a dog.

Verse 6:
The dog takes a cat,
The dog takes a cat,
Heigh-ho, the derry-o,
The dog takes a cat.

Verse 7:
The cat takes a rat,
The cat takes a rat,
Heigh-ho, the derry-o,
The cat takes a rat.

Verse 8:
The rat takes a cheese,
The rat takes a cheese,
Heigh-ho, the derry-o,
The rat takes a cheese.

Verse 9:
The cheese stands alone,
The cheese stands alone,
Heigh-ho, the derry-o,
The cheese stands alone.

FATHER'S WHISKERS

TRADITIONAL

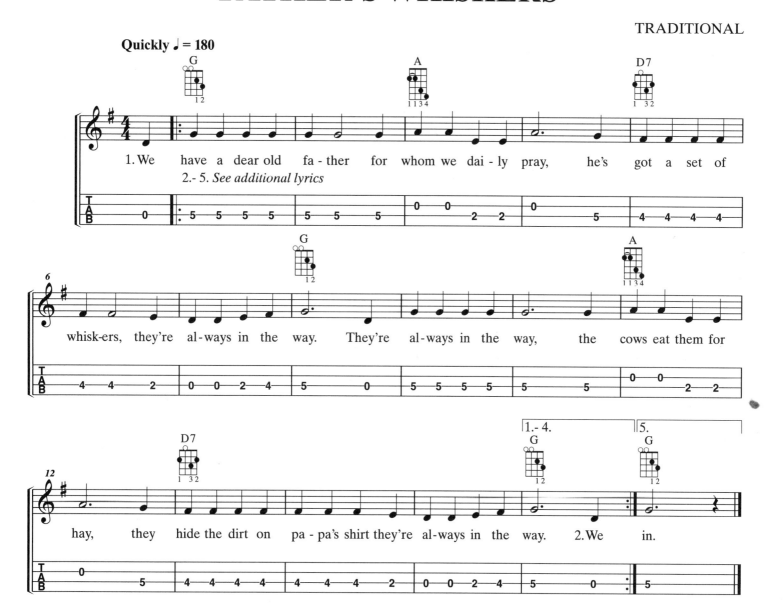

Quickly ♩ = 180

1. We have a dear old fa-ther for whom we dai-ly pray, he's got a set of
2.- 5. *See additional lyrics*

whisk-ers, they're al-ways in the way. They're al-ways in the way, the cows eat them for

hay, they hide the dirt on pa-pa's shirt they're al-ways in the way. 2. We in.

Verse 2:
We have a dear old brother,
He's got a Ford machine,
He uses Father's whiskers
To strain the gasoline.
To strain the gasoline,
To strain the gasoline,
He uses Father's whiskers
To strain the gasoline.

Verse 3:
Around the supper table,
We make a merry group,
Until dear Father's whiskers
Get tangled in the soup.
Get tangled in the soup,
Get tangled in the soup,
Until dear Father's whiskers
Get tangled in the soup.

Verse 4:
When Father's in a tavern,
He likes his lager beer,
He pins a pretzel on his nose
To keep his whiskers clear.
To keep his whiskers clear,
To keep his whiskers clear,
He pins a pretzel on his nose
To keep his whiskers clear.

Verse 5:
When Father goes in swimming,
No bathing suit for him,
He ties his whiskers 'round his waist,
And then he jumps right in.
And then he jumps right in,
And then he jumps right in,
He ties his whiskers 'round his waist
And then he jumps right in.

FOUND A PEANUT

(To the tune of "Clementine")

TRADITIONAL

Moderately ♩ = 120

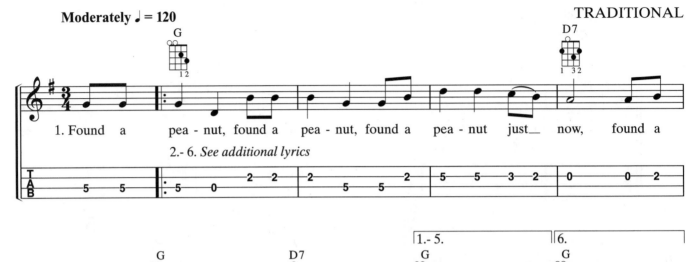

1. Found a pea-nut, found a pea-nut, found a pea-nut just__ now, found a

2.- 6. *See additional lyrics*

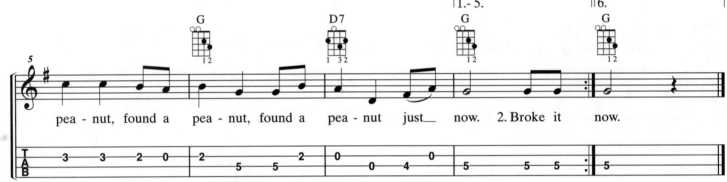

pea-nut, found a pea-nut, found a pea-nut just__ now. 2. Broke it now.

Verse 2:
Broke it open, broke it open,
Broke it open just now,
Broke it open, broke it open,
Broke it open just now.

Verse 3:
It was rotten, it was rotten,
It was rotten just now,
It was rotten, it was rotten,
It was rotten just now.

Verse 4:
Ate it anyway, ate it anyway,
Ate it anyway just now,
Ate it anyway, ate it anyway,
Ate it anyway just now.

Verse 2:
Broke it open, broke it open,
Broke it open just now,
Broke it open, broke it open,
Broke it open just now.

Verse 3:
It was rotten, it was rotten,
It was rotten just now,
It was rotten, it was rotten,
It was rotten just now.

Verse 4:
Ate it anyway, ate it anyway,
Ate it anyway just now,
Ate it anyway, ate it anyway,
Ate it anyway just now.

GO IN AND OUT THE WINDOW

TRADITIONAL

Moderately fast ♩ = 140

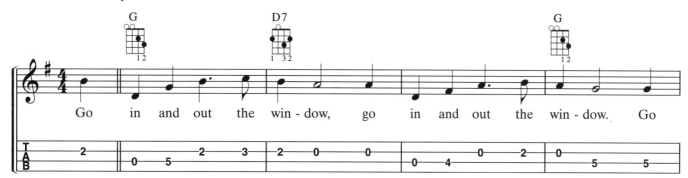

Go in and out the win-dow, go in and out the win-dow. Go

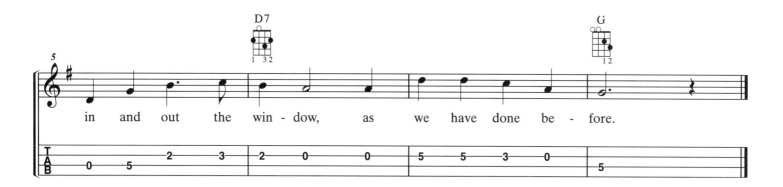

in and out the win-dow, as we have done be-fore.

Make up additional verses, for example:

Let's strum the ukulele,
The guitar and mandolin.
We'll pick a little banjo
As we laugh and sing.

Let's have some milk and cookies,
Let's have some milk and cookies,
Let's have some milk and cookies,
And then we'll have some more.

FRÈRE JACQUES

TRADITIONAL

Moderately ♩ = 140

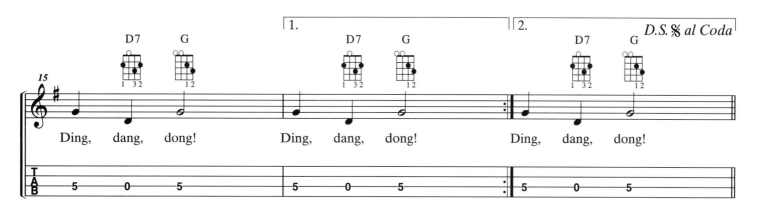

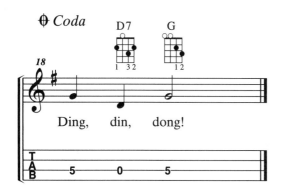

Verse 2:
Wake up! Wake up! Wake up! Wake up!
Brother John! Brother John!
Ring the morning matins,
Ring the morning matins,
Ding, dang, dong!
Ding, dang, dong!
(To Chorus:)

GOODBYE, MY LOVER, GOODBYE

TRADITIONAL

Moderately ♪ = 130

Verse:

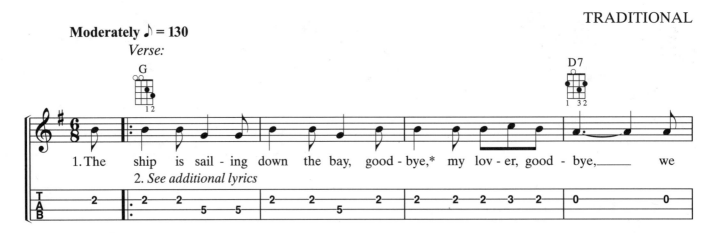

1. The ship is sail - ing down the bay, good - bye,* my lov - er, good - bye,_____ we

2. *See additional lyrics*

may not meet for man - y a day, good - bye, my lov - er, good - bye. Sing - ing

Chorus:

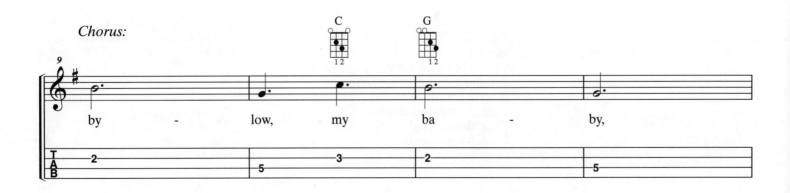

by - low, my ba - by,

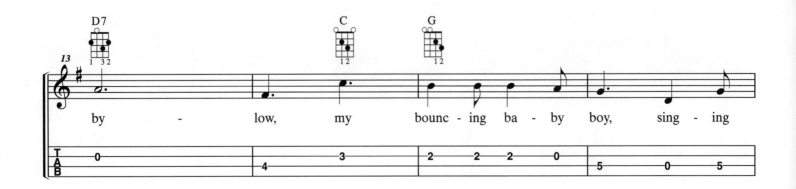

by - low, my bounc - ing ba - by boy, sing - ing

*When sung as a lullaby, try substituting the word "goodnight" for "goodbye" and "baby" for "lover."

Goodbye, My Lover, Goodbye - 2 - 1

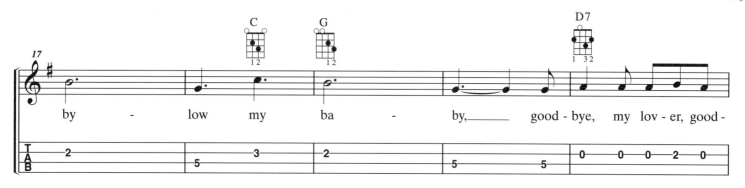

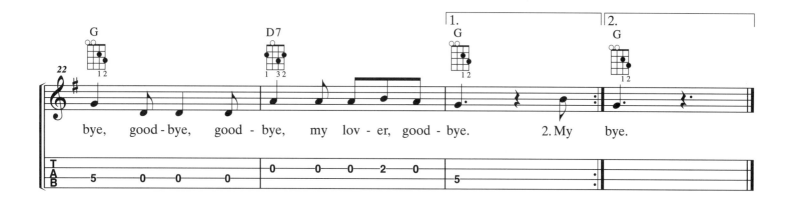

Verse 2:
My heart will ever more be true,
Goodbye, my lover, goodbye,
Tho now I sadly bid you adieu,
Goodbye, my lover, goodbye.
(To Chorus:)

GOODNIGHT, LADIES

(To the tune of "Merrily We Roll Along")

TRADITIONAL

Verse 2:
Farewell, ladies,
Farewell, ladies,
Farewell, ladies,
We're going to leave you now.
(To Chorus:)

Verse 3:
Sweet dreams, ladies,
Sweet dreams, ladies,
Sweet dreams, ladies,
We're going to leave you now.
(To Chorus:)

Verse 4:
Sweet dreams, baby,
Sweet dreams, baby,
Sweet dreams, baby,
It's time to say goodnight.

Chorus 4:
Softly now we go to sleep,
Go to sleep, go to sleep,
Gently now we go to sleep,
It's time to say goodnight.

HERE WE GO 'ROUND
THE MULBERRY BUSH

TRADITIONAL

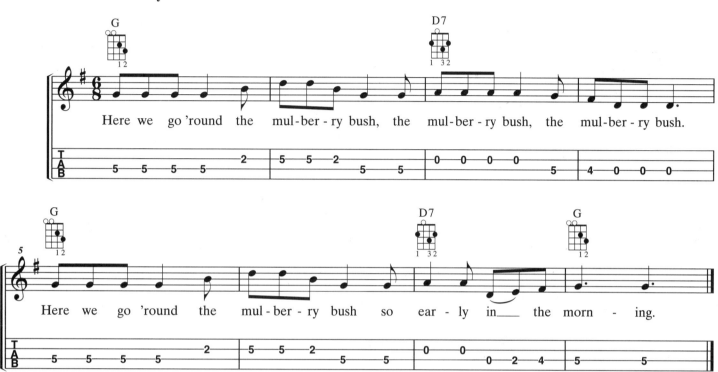

There are many add-on lyrics. Here are just a few.

This is the way we wash our clothes,
Wash our clothes, wash our clothes.
This is the way we wash our clothes
So early Monday morning.

This is the way we iron our clothes,
we iron our clothes, we iron our clothes.
This is the way we iron our clothes
So early Tuesday morning.

This is the way we mend out clothes,
we mend out clothes, we mend out clothes.
This is the way we mend out clothes
So early Wednesday morning.

Sweep the floor…

Scrub the floor…

Wash our face…

Comb our hair…

Shine our shoes…

Go to school…

Brush our teeth…

Bake our bread…

Clap our hands…

HICKORY DICKORY DOCK

TRADITIONAL

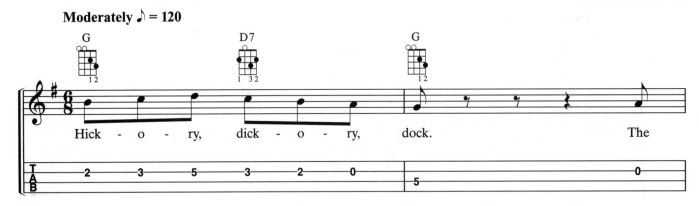

Hick - o - ry, dick - o - ry, dock. The

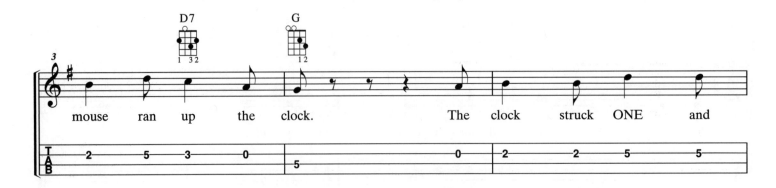

mouse ran up the clock. The clock struck ONE and

down he run, hick - o - ry, dick - o - ry, dock.

HUSH, LITTLE BABY

TRADITIONAL

Moderately ♩ = 120

1. Hush, Lit - tle ba - by, don't say a word,
2.- 7. *See additional lyrics*

ma - ma's gon - na buy you a mock - ing bird. ba - by in town.

Verse 2:
If that mockingbird word won't sing,
Mama's gonna buy you a diamond ring.

Verse 3:
If that ring is made of brass,
Mama's gonna buy you a looking glass.

Verse 4:
If that looking glass gets broke,
Mama's gonna buy you and ox and yoke.

Verse 5:
If that ox and yoke turn over,
Mama's gonna buy you a dog named Rover.

Verse 6:
If that dog named Rover runs away,
Mama's gonna buy you a horse and sleigh.

Verse 7:
If that horse and sleigh break down,
You'll still be the cutest little baby in town.

I HAVE A LITTLE DREIDEL

TRADITIONAL

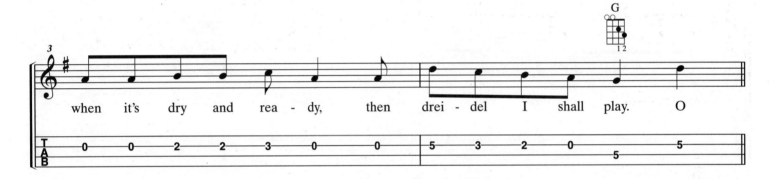

IF YOU'RE HAPPY

(And You Know It)

TRADITIONAL

Verse 2:
If you're happy and you know it, WIGGLE YOUR EARS.
If you're happy and you know it, wiggle your ears.
If you're happy and you know it
Then your ears will surely show it,
If you're happy and you know it, wiggle your ears.

Verse 3:
If you're happy and you know it, BLINK YOUR EYES.
If you're happy and you know it, blink your eyes.
If you're happy and you know it
Then your eyes will surely show it,
If you're happy and you know it, blink your eyes.

Verse 4:
If you're happy and you know it, TOUCH YOUR NOSE, etc.

Verse 5:
If you're happy and you know it, PULL YOUR EARS, etc.

Verse 6:
If you're happy and you know it, STAMP YOUR FEET, etc.

IT'S RAINING, IT'S POURING

TRADITIONAL

Moderately fast ♩ = 150

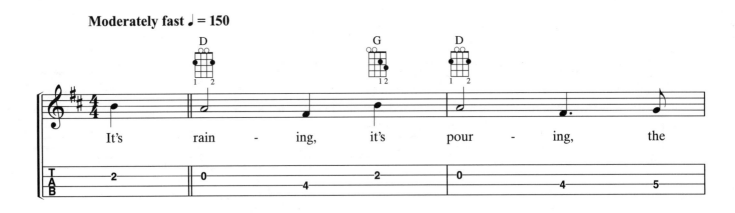

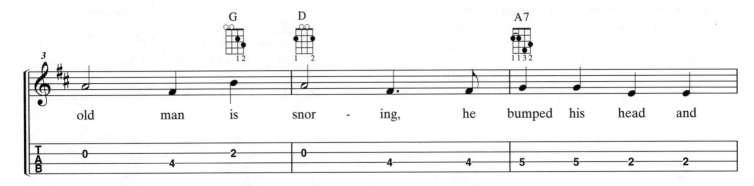

ITSY BITSY SPIDER

Moderately fast ♪ = 140

TRADITIONAL

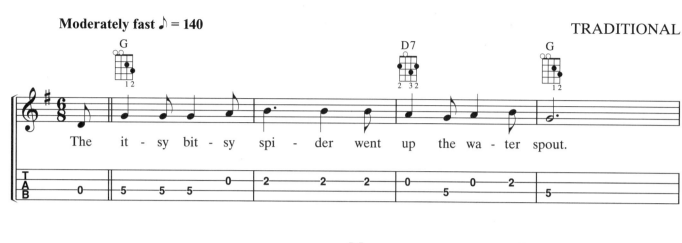

The it - sy bit - sy spi - der went up the wa - ter spout.

Down came the rain_____ and washed the spi - der out.

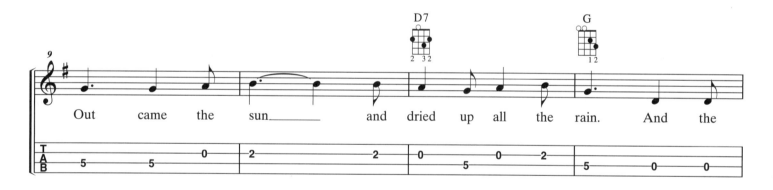

Out came the sun_____ and dried up all the rain. And the

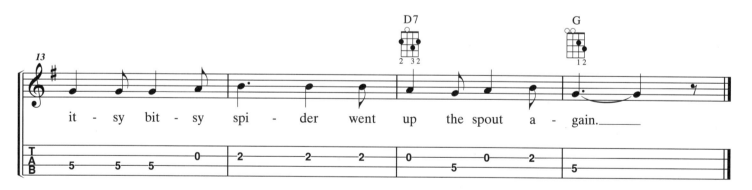

it - sy bit - sy spi - der went up the spout a - gain._____

JESUS LOVES ME

Words by
ANNA BARTLETT WARNER

TRADITIONAL HYMN

JOHN BROWN'S BABY

TRADITIONAL

LIMERICKS

Quickly ♩ = 175

1. There once was a la - dy from Ni - ger,_____ who rode on the
2. - 7. *See additional lyrics*

back of a ti - ger._____ They re - turned from a ride, with the la - dy in -

side, and a smile on the face of the ti - ger._____ There ____

Verse 2:
There once was two cats from Kilkenny,
Each thought that was one cat was too many.
So they started to fight,
And to scratch and to bite,
Now instead of two cats there aren't any.

Verse 3:
There once was a man from Peru,
Who dreamed he was eating his shoe.
He awoke in the night
With a terrible fright,
And found it was actually true.

Verse 4:
A mouse in her room woke Miss Dowd,
She was frightened it must be allowed,
But a happy thought hit her
To scare off the critter,
She sat up in the bed and meowed.

Verse 5:
There once was a girl who said, "Why
Can't I look in my ear with my eye?
If I put my mind to it,
I surely can do it,
You never can tell till you try."

Verse 6:
There once was a girl in the choir,
Whose voice rang higher and higher,
It reached such a height
It went clear out of sight,
And they found it next day in the spire.

Verse 7:
There was a young lady from Lynn,
Who was so excessively thin,
That when she essayed
To drink lemonade,
She looked down the straw and fell in.

LONDON BRIDGE IS FALLING DOWN

TRADITIONAL

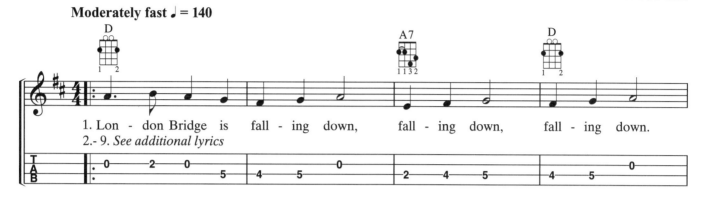

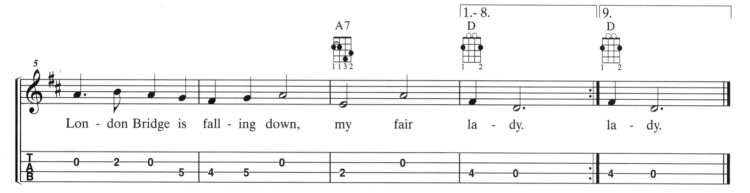

Verse 2:
How shall it be built again, built again, built again?
How shall it be built again,
My fair lady?

Verse 3:
Build it up with gravel and stone, etc.

Verse 4:
Gravel and stone will wash away, etc.

Verse 5:
Build it up with iron and steel, etc.

Verse 6:
Iron and steel will bend and bow, etc.

Verse 7:
Build it up with silver and gold, etc.

Verse 8:
Thieves will steal the silver and gold, etc.

Verse 9:
Then we'll send a man to watch, etc.

MARY HAD A LITTLE LAMB

TRADITIONAL

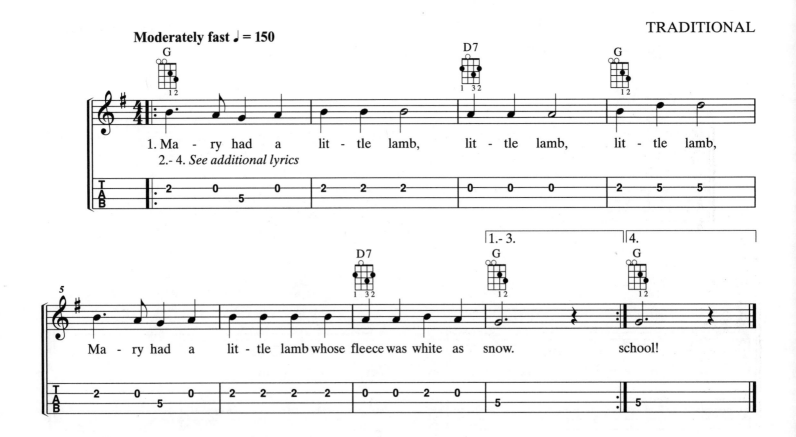

Verse 2:
Ev'rywhere that Mary went,
Mary went, Mary, went,
Ev'rywhere that Mary went
The lamb was sure to go.

Verse 3:
It followed her to school one day,
School one day, school one day.
It followed her to school one day
Which was against the rule.

Verse 4:
It made the children laugh and play,
Laugh and play, laugh and play.
It made the children laugh and play
To see a lamb at school.

MICHAEL FINNEGAN

TRADITIONAL

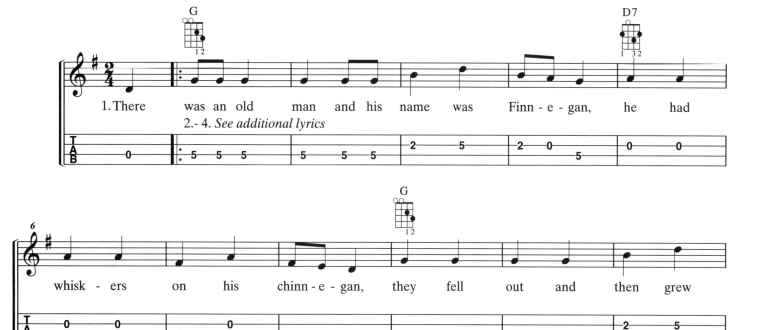

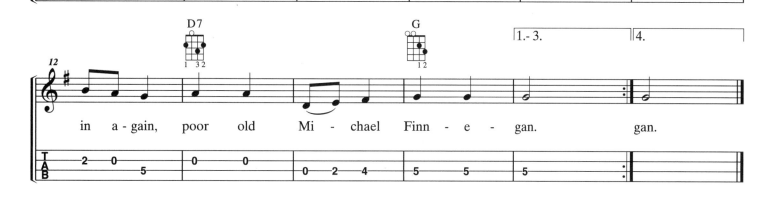

Verse 2:
There was an old man and his name was Finnegan,
He went fishing with a pinnegan,
Caught a fish and threw it in again,
Poor old Michael Finnegan.

Verse 3:
There was an old man and his name was Finnegan,
He grew fat and then grew thin again,
Then he died and had to begin again,
Poor old Michael Finnegan.

Verse 4:
I had a cat and his name was Finnegan,
He had whiskers on his chinnegan,
He'd want out and then want in again,
My old kitty cat Finnegan.

MIGHTY LAK' A ROSE

Words by
FRANK L. STANTON

Music by
ETHELBERT NEVIN

Mighty Lak' a Rose - 2 - 1

MR. FROG WENT A-COURTING

TRADITIONAL

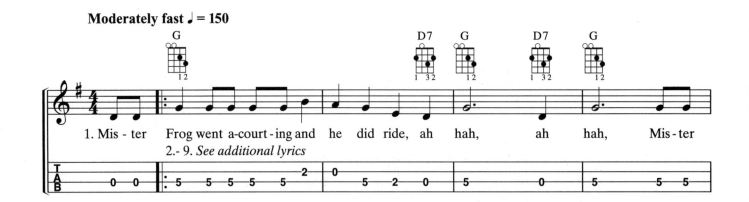

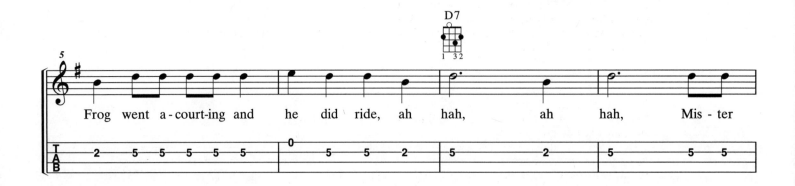

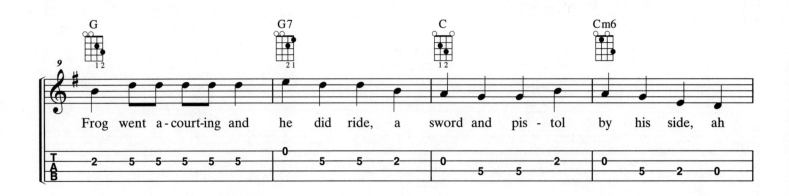

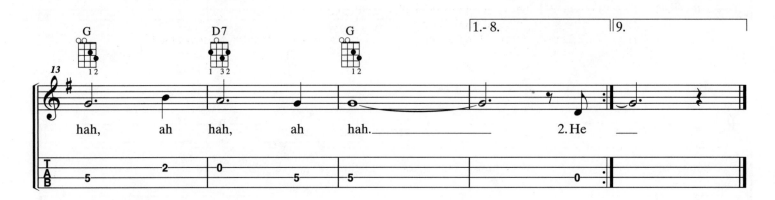

Mr. Frog Went A-Courting - 2 - 1

Verse 2:
He rode up to Miss Mousie's door, ah hah, ah hah,
He rode up to Miss Mousie's door, ah hah, ah hah,
He rode up to Miss Mousie's door, gave three knocks and then one more,
Ah hah, ah hah, ah hah.

Verse 3:
He said, "Miss Mousie are you within?" ah hah, ah hah,
He said, "Miss Mousie are you within?" ah hah, ah hah,
She said, "Mr. Frog I sit and spin, just lift the latch and please come in."
Ah hah, ah hah, ah hah.

Verse 4:
He put Miss Mousie upon his knee, ah hah, ah hah,
He put Miss Mousie upon his knee, ah hah, ah hah,
He put Miss Mousie on his knee, he said, "Missy Mouse will you marry me?"
Ah hah, ah hah, ah hah.

Verse 5:
"Without my Uncle Rat's consent, ah hah, ah hah,
Without my Uncle Rat's consent, ah hah, ah hah,
Without my Uncle Rat's consent I wouldn't marry the president."
Ah hah, ah hah, ah hah.

Verse 6:
Where will the wedding supper be? ah hah, ah hah,
Where will the wedding supper be? ah hah, ah hah,
Where will the wedding supper be? Way down yonder in a hollow tree.
Ah hah, ah hah, ah hah.

Verse 7:
What will the wedding supper be? ah hah, ah hah,
What will the wedding supper be? ah hah, ah hah,
What will the wedding supper be? Two green beans and a black-eyed pea.
Ah hah, ah hah, ah hah.

Verse 8:
They all went swimming across the lake, ah hah, ah hah,
They all went swimming across the lake, ah hah, ah hah,
They all went swimming across the lake, they all got swallowed by a big black snake.
Ah hah, ah hah, ah hah.

Verse 9:
There's bread and cheese upon the shelf, ah hah, ah hah,
There's bread and cheese upon the shelf, ah hah, ah hah,
There's bread and cheese upon the shelf, if you want any more you better get it yourself.
Ah hah, ah hah, ah hah.

THE MUFFIN MAN

TRADITIONAL

Verse 2:
Yes, I know the muffin man,
The muffin man, the muffin man.
Yes, I know the muffin man
Who lives in Drury Lane.

Verse 3:
Yes, we know the muffin man,
The muffin man, the muffin man.
Yes, we know the muffin man
Who lives in Drury Lane.

NINETY-NINE BOTTLES OF BEER

TRADITIONAL

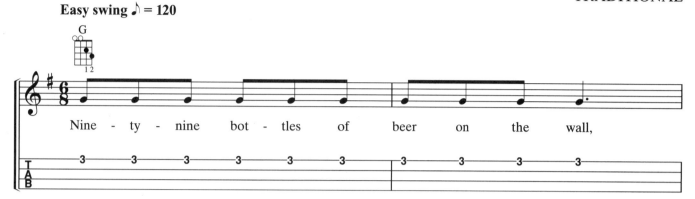

Nine - ty - nine bot - tles of beer on the wall,

nine - ty - nine bot - tles of beer,_____ if one of those bot - tles should

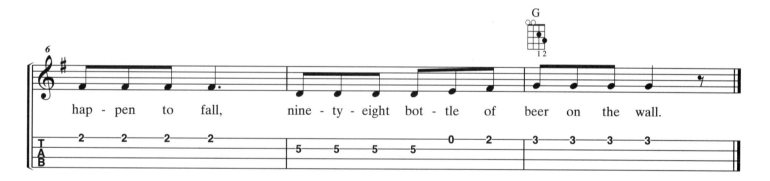

hap - pen to fall, nine - ty - eight bot - tle of beer on the wall.

And so on, counting backwards and reducing the number of bottles by one each time.

MY BONNIE LIES OVER THE OCEAN

Moderately fast ♩ = 150

SCOTTISH TRADITIONAL

Verse:

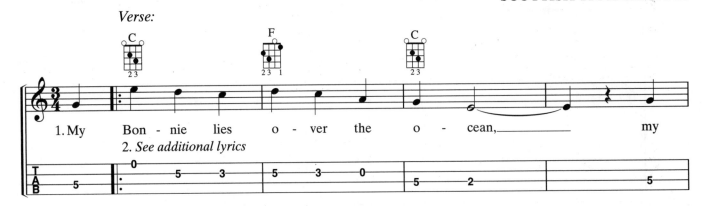

1. My Bon - nie lies o - ver the o - cean,_____ my
2. *See additional lyrics*

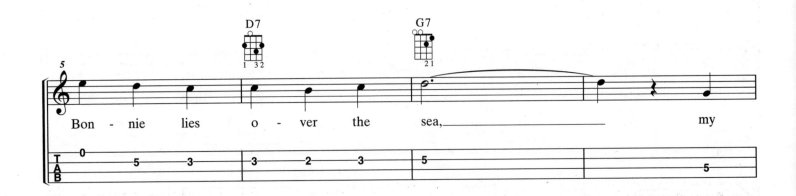

Bon - nie lies o - ver the sea,_____ my

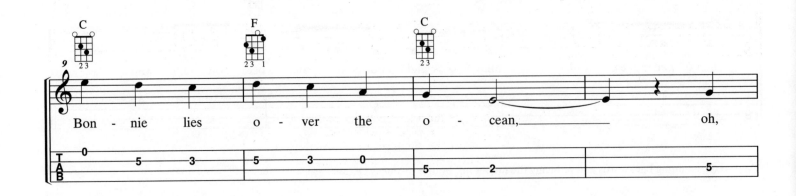

Bon - nie lies o - ver the o - cean,_____ oh,

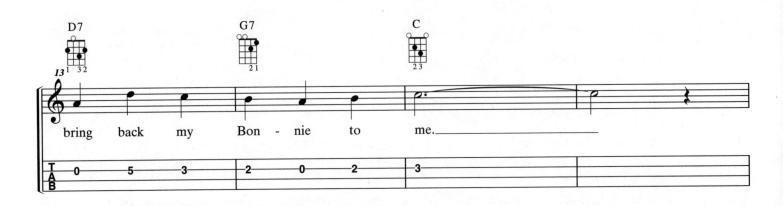

bring back my Bon - nie to me._____

My Bonnie Lies Over the Ocean - 2 - 1

Chorus:

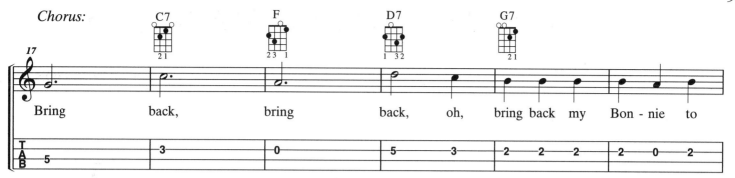

Bring back, bring back, oh, bring back my Bon - nie to

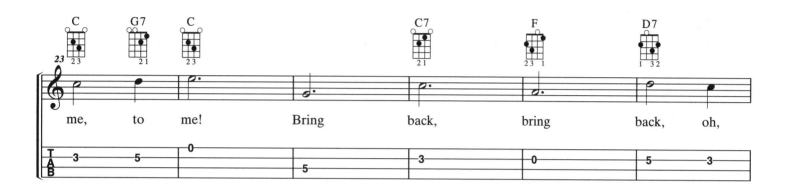

me, to me! Bring back, bring back, oh,

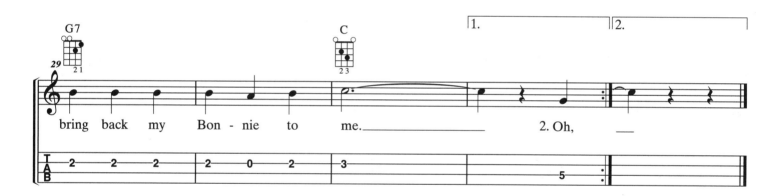

bring back my Bon - nie to me._____ 2. Oh, ___

Verse 2:
Oh, blow the winds over the ocean,
Oh, blow the winds over the sea,
Oh, blow the winds over the ocean,
And bring back my Bonnie to me.
(To Chorus:)

A fun group activity for this song is divided into two parts:

Part 1) When the word "Bonnie" is first sung, everyone stands. As the song continues, everyone sits down on the word "Bonnie." This action is repeated until the end of the song, standing up and sitting down.

Part 2) Now the song begins again. When a word beginning with "B" is sung, everyone stands. When the next "B" is sung, everyone sits down. This action is repeated until the end of the song, up and down.

The song at first may be sung slowly. As it repeats, it gets faster and faster until absolute chaos results!

POLLY WOLLY DOODLE

Moderately fast ♩ = 150

TRADITIONAL

Verse:

1. Oh, I went down South for to see my Sal, sing Pol - ly wol - ly doo - dle all the

2.-5. *See additional lyrics*

day, my Sal, she am a spunk - y gal, sing

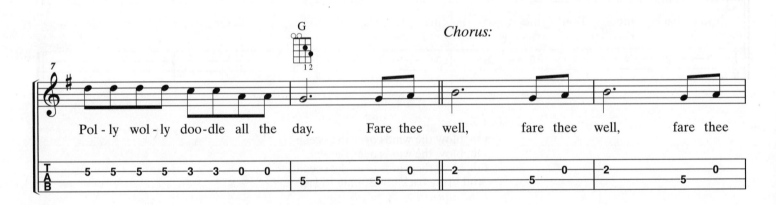

Chorus:

Pol - ly wol - ly doo - dle all the day. Fare thee well, fare thee well, fare thee

well my fair - y fay, for I'm go'n' to Lou - si - an - na for to

see my Su - sy - an - na, sing   Pol - ly wol - ly doo-dle all the day.   2. Oh,   my   day.

Verse 2:
Oh, my Sal she is a maiden fair,
Sing Polly wolly doodle all the day,
With curly eyes and laughing hair,
Sing Polly wolly doodle all the day.
(To Chorus:)

Verse 3:
Down behind the barn on my hands and knees,
Sing Polly wolly doodle all the day,
I thought I heard a chicken sneeze,
Sing Polly wolly doodle all the day.
(To Chorus:)

Verse 4:
He sneezed so hard with the whooping cough,
Sing Polly wolly doodle all the day,
He sneezed his head and tail right off,
Sing Polly wolly doodle all the day.
(To Chorus:)

Verse 5:
Oh, a grasshopper sitting on a railroad track,
Sing Polly wolly doodle all the day,
A-picking his teeth with a carpet tack,
Sing Polly wolly doodle all the day.
(To Chorus:)

ON THE BRIDGE OF AVIGNON
(Sur Le Pont D'Avignon)

TRADITIONAL

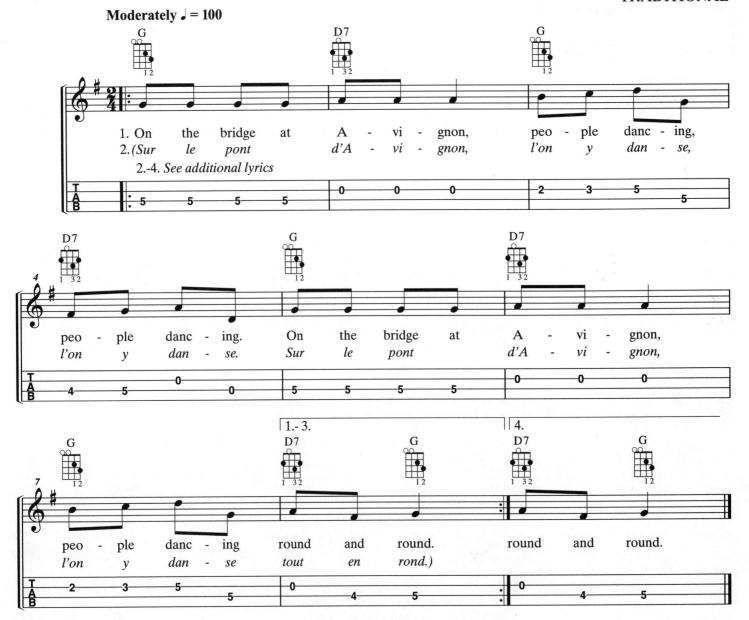

Verse 2:
On the bridge at Avignon,
Soldiers dancing, soldiers dancing,
On the bridge at Avignon,
Soldiers dancing round and round.

Verse 3:
On the bridge at Avignon,
Ladies dancing, ladies dancing,
On the bridge of Avignon,
Ladies dancing round and round.

Verse 4:
On the bridge at Avignon,
Children dancing, children dancing,
On the bridge at Avignon,
Children dancing round and round.

POP! GOES THE WEASEL

TRADITIONAL

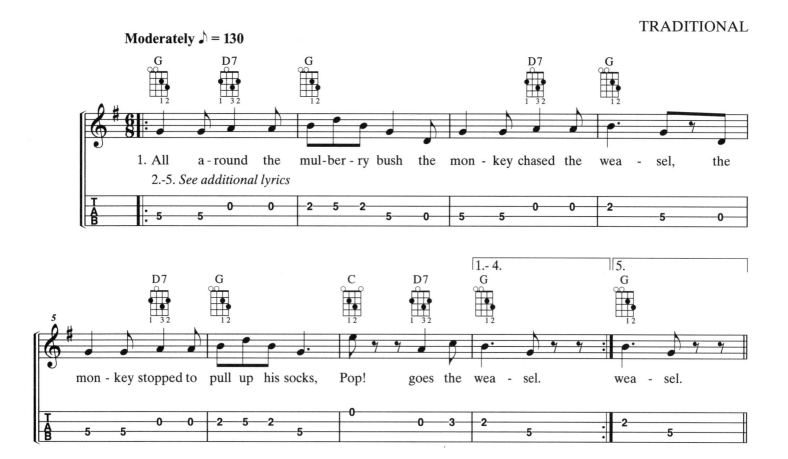

Verse 2:
Ev'ry night when I get home
The monkey's on the table,
Go get a stick and knock him off,
Pop! goes the weasel.

Verse 3:
A penny for a spool of thread,
A penny for a needle,
That's the way the money goes,
Pop! goes the weasel.

Verse 4:
Mary's got the whooping cough
And Dicky's got the measels,
That's the way the money goes,
Pop! goes the weasel.

Verse 5:
Half a pound of tuppeny rice,
Half a pound of treacle,
Mix it up and shake it twice,
Pop! goes the weasel.

RAISINS AND ALMONDS

Words and Music by
ABRAHAM GOLDFADEN

RIG-A-JIG-JIG

TRADITIONAL

RING AROUND THE ROSIE

TRADITIONAL

Ring a-round a ros - ie, a pock - et full of pos - ies,

ash - es! ash - es! we all fall down.

ROCK-A-BYE-BABY

TRADITIONAL

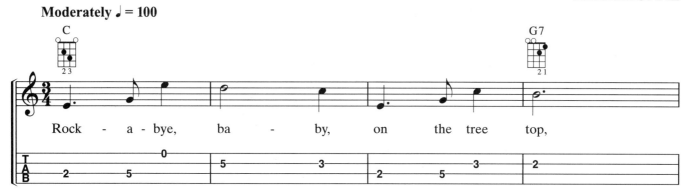

Rock - a - bye, ba - by, on the tree top,

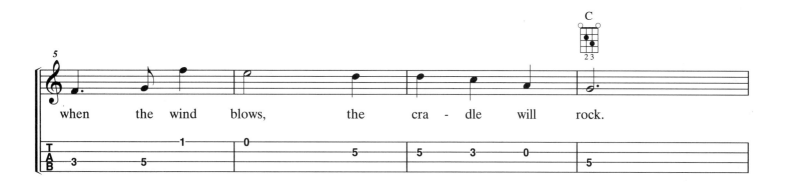

when the wind blows, the cra - dle will rock.

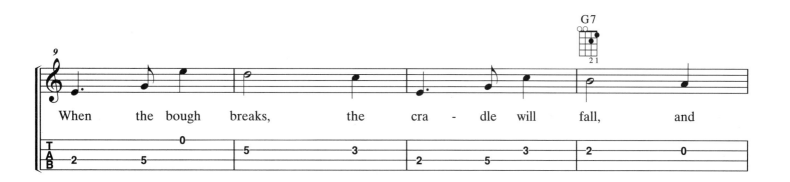

When the bough breaks, the cra - dle will fall, and

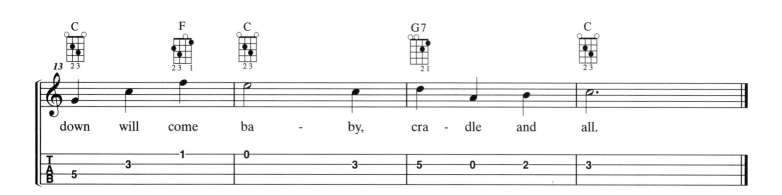

down will come ba - by, cra - dle and all.

ROW, ROW, ROW YOUR BOAT

TRADITIONAL

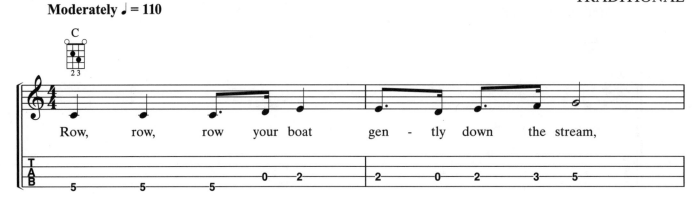

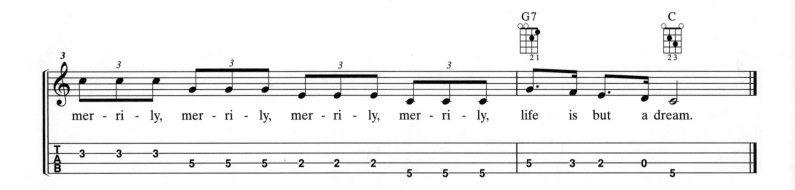

SAILING, SAILING

TRADITIONAL

Moderately fast ♪ = 150

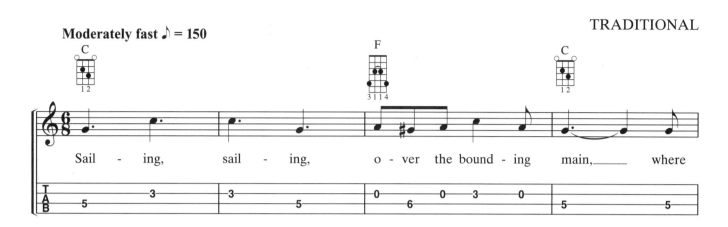

Sail - ing, sail - ing, o - ver the bound - ing main,_____ where

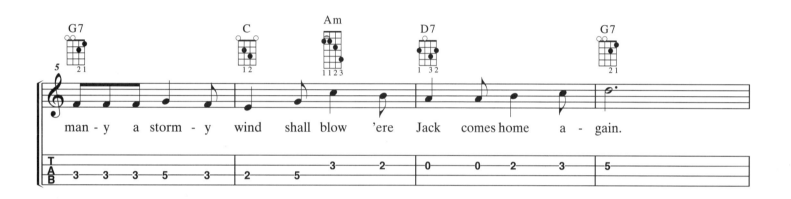

man - y a storm - y wind shall blow 'ere Jack comes home a - gain.

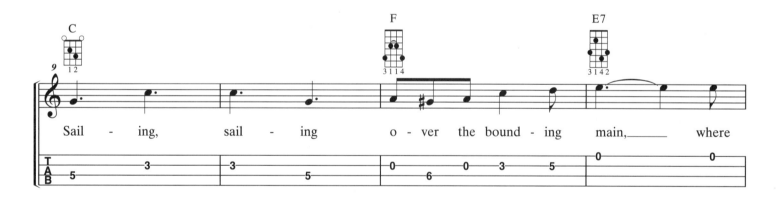

Sail - ing, sail - ing o - ver the bound - ing main,_____ where

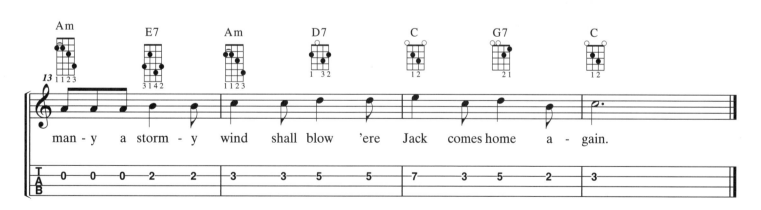

man - y a storm - y wind shall blow 'ere Jack comes home a - gain.

SHE'LL BE COMING 'ROUND THE MOUNTAIN

TRADITIONAL

Moderately ♩ = 110

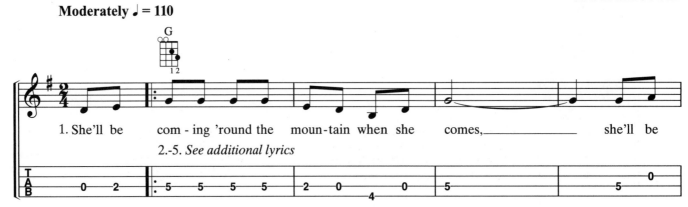

1. She'll be com-ing 'round the moun-tain when she comes,___ she'll be

2.-5. *See additional lyrics*

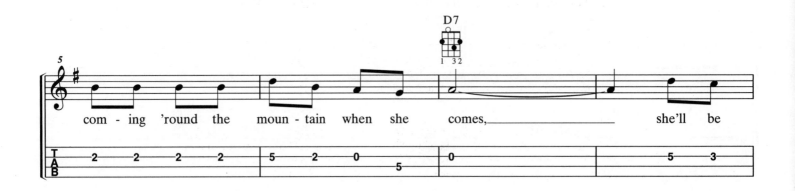

com-ing 'round the moun-tain when she comes,___ she'll be

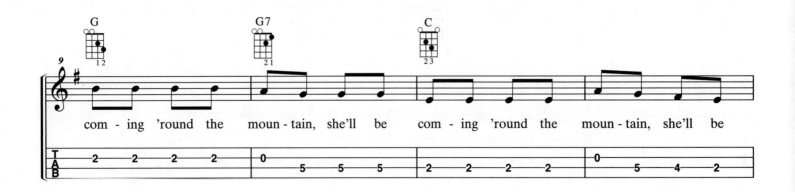

com-ing 'round the moun-tain, she'll be com-ing 'round the moun-tain, she'll be

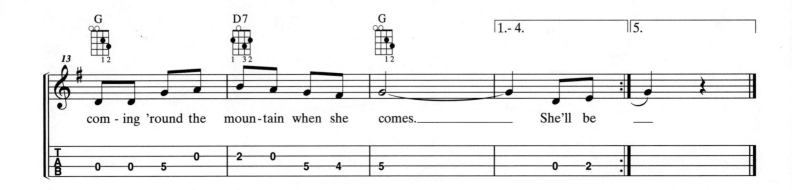

com-ing 'round the moun-tain when she comes.___ She'll be

She'll Be Coming 'Round the Mountain - 2 - 1

Verse 1:
She'll be coming 'round the mountain when she comes, (TOOT, TOOT)
She'll be coming 'round the mountain when she comes, (TOOT, TOOT)
She'll be coming ' round the mountain, she'll be coming 'round the mountain,
She'll be coming 'round the moutain when she comes. (TOOT, TOOT)

Verse 2:
She'll be pulling six white horses when she comes, (WHOA, HORSE)
She'll be pulling six white horses when she comes, (WHOA, HORSE)
She'll be pulling six white horses, she'll be pulling six white horses,
She'll be pulling six white horse when she comes. (WHOA, HORSE)

Verse 3:
We'll all come out to meet her when she comes, (HOWDY DOO)
We'll all come out to meet her when she comes, (HOWDY DOO)
We'll all come out to meet her, we'll all come out to meet her,
We'll all come out to meet her when she comes. (HOWDY DOO)

Verse 4:
She'll be wearing wool pajamas when she comes, (SCRATCH, SCRATCH)
She'll be wearing wool pajamas when she comes, (SCRATCH, SCRATCH)
She'll be wearing wool pajamas, she'll be wearing wool pajamas,
She'll be wearing wool pajamas when she comes. (SCRATCH, SCRATCH)

Verse 5:
She'll have to sleep with Grandma when she comes, (SNORE, SNORE)
She'll have to sleep with Grandma when she comes, (SNORE, SNORE)
She'll have to sleep with Grandma, she'll have to sleep with Grandma,
She'll have to sleep with Grandma when she comes. (SNORE, SNORE)

And then as a grand finale:
TOOT, TOOT
WHOA, HORSE
HOWDY DOO
SCRATCH, SCRATCH
SNORE, SNORE

SKIP TO MY LOU

TRADITIONAL

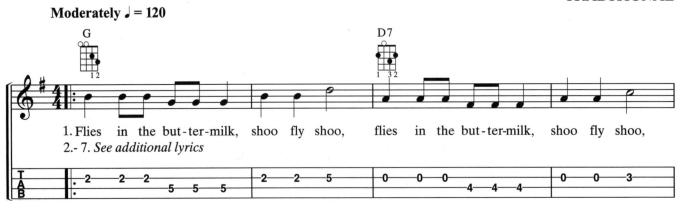

1. Flies in the but-ter-milk, shoo fly shoo, flies in the but-ter-milk, shoo fly shoo,
2.- 7. *See additional lyrics*

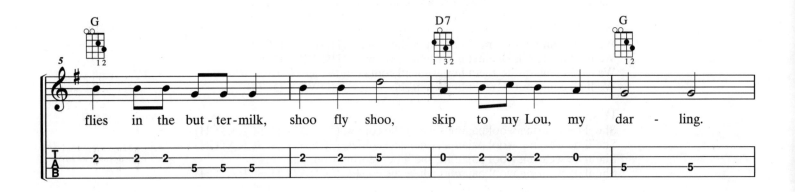

flies in the but-ter-milk, shoo fly shoo, skip to my Lou, my dar - ling.

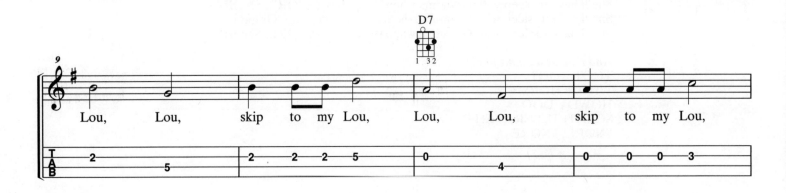

Lou, Lou, skip to my Lou, Lou, Lou, skip to my Lou,

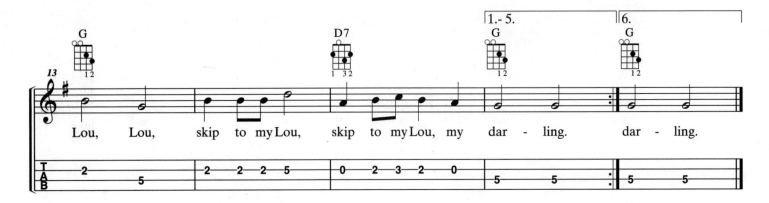

Lou, Lou, skip to my Lou, skip to my Lou, my dar - ling. dar - ling.

Skip to My Lou - 2 - 1

Verse 2:
Lost my partner, what'll I do?
Lost my partner, what'll I do?
Lost my partner, what'll I do?
Skip to my Lou, my darling.

Verse 3:
I'll find another one prettier than you,
I'll find another one prettier than you,
I'll find another one prettier than you,
Skip to my Lou, my darling.

Verse 4:
Little red wagon painted blue,
Little red wagon painted blue,
Little red wagon painted blue,
Skip to my Lou, my darling.

Verse 5:
Cat's in the cream jar, what'll I do,
Cat's in the cream jar, what'll I do,
Cat's in the cream jar, what'll I do,
Skip to my Lou, my darling.

Verse 6:
Come again, skip to my Lou,
Come again, skip to my Lou,
Come again, skip to my Lou,
Skip to my Lou, my darling.

Verse 7:
Dog ate my pancakes, what'll I do?
Dog ate my pancakes, what'll I do?
Dog ate my pancakes, what'll I do?
Skip to my Lou, my darling.

SING A SONG OF SIXPENCE

TRADITIONAL

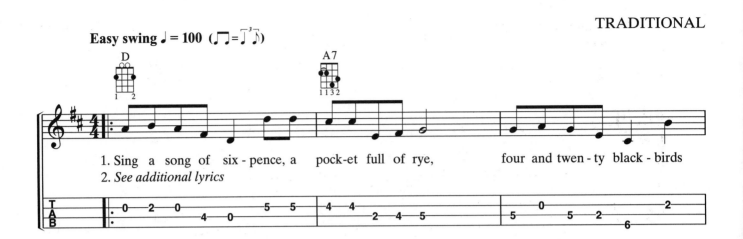

1. Sing a song of six - pence, a pock-et full of rye, four and twen - ty black - birds
2. *See additional lyrics*

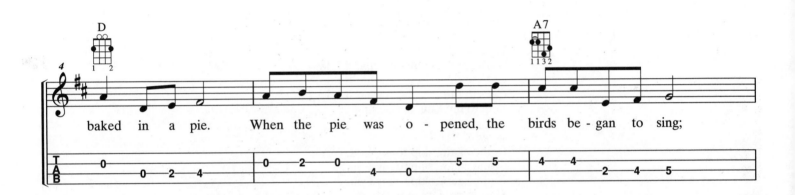

baked in a pie. When the pie was o - pened, the birds be - gan to sing;

was - n't that a dain - ty dish to set be - fore the king. pecked_ off her nose.

Verse 2:
The king was in his counting house, counting out his money,
The queen was in the parlor eating bread and honey.
The maid was in the garden hanging out the clothes,
When down came a blackbird and pecked off her nose.

THIS OLD MAN

Moderately fast ♩ = 160

TRADITIONAL

1. This old man, he plays ONE, he plays knick-knack on my drum, with a
2.-10. *See additional lyrics*

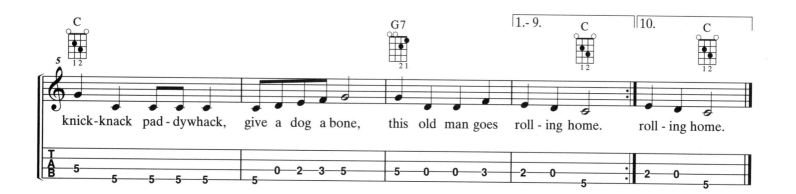

knick-knack pad-dywhack, give a dog a bone, this old man goes roll-ing home. roll-ing home.

Verse 2:
This old man, he played TWO,
He played knick, knack on my shoe, etc.

Verse 3:
This old man, he played THREE,
He played knick-knack on my tree, etc.

Verse 4:
This old man, he played FOUR,
He played knick-knack on my door, etc.

Verse 5:
This old man, he played FIVE,
He played knick-knack on my hive, etc.

Verse 6:
This old man, he played SIX,
He played knick-knack on my sticks, etc.

Verse 7:
This old man, he played SEVEN,
He played knick-knack up in heaven, etc.

Verse 8:
This old man, he played EIGHT,
He played knick-knack on my gate, etc.

Verse 9:
This old man, he played NINE,
He played knick-knack on my vine, etc.

Verse 10:
This old man, he played TEN,
Then he started all over again, etc.

THREE BLIND MICE

Moderately fast ♪ = 130

TRADITIONAL

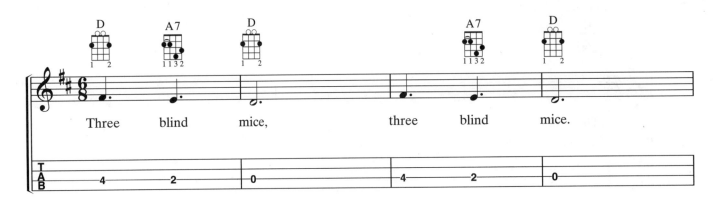

Three blind mice, three blind mice.

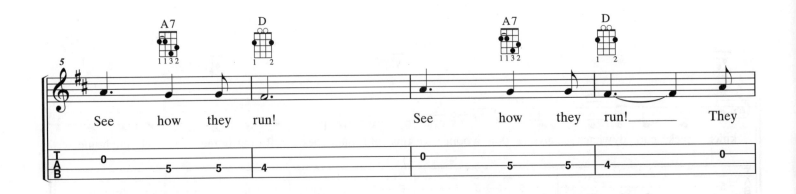

See how they run! See how they run!_____ They

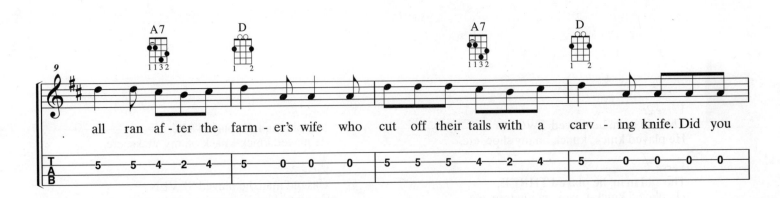

all ran af - ter the farm - er's wife who cut off their tails with a carv - ing knife. Did you

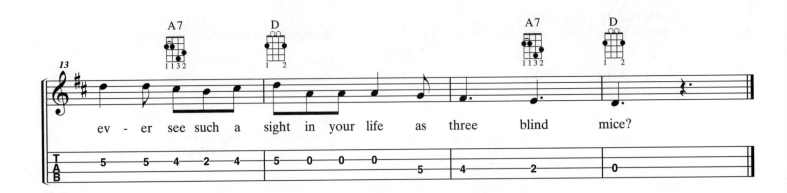

ev - er see such a sight in your life as three blind mice?

TWINKLE, TWINKLE, LITTLE STAR

TRADITIONAL

Moderately ♩ = 130

OH WHERE, OH WHERE, HAS MY LITTLE DOG GONE?

Words and Music by
SEPTIMUS WINNER

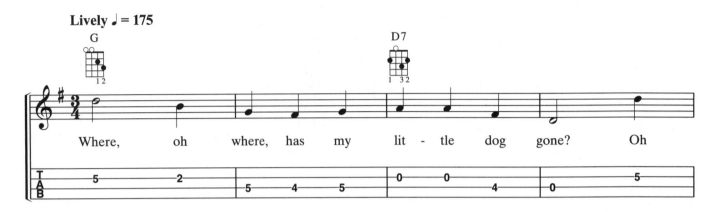

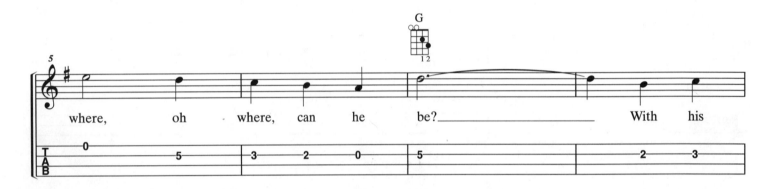

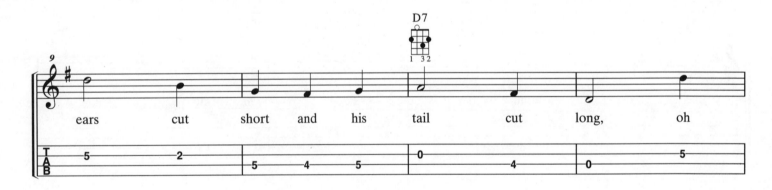

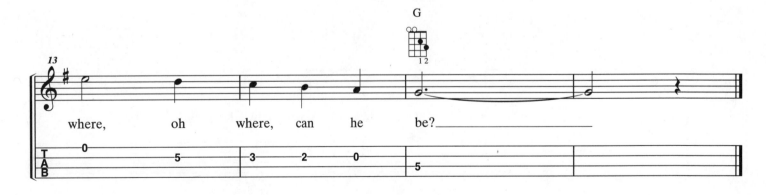

MANDOLIN CHORD DICTIONARY

A CHORDS

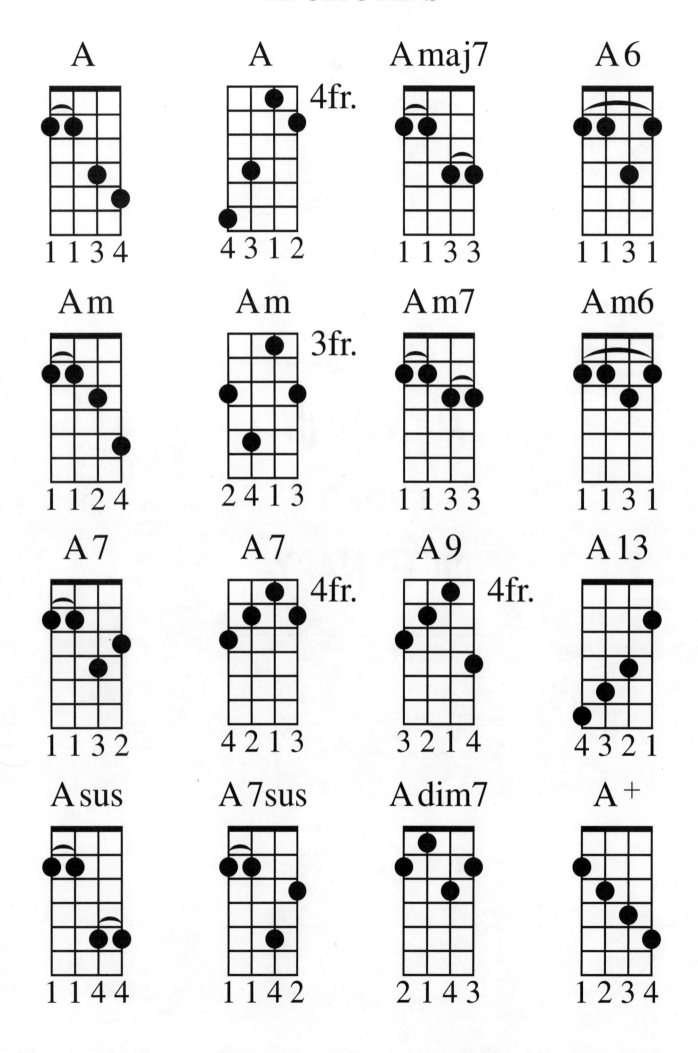

B♭ (A♯) CHORDS*

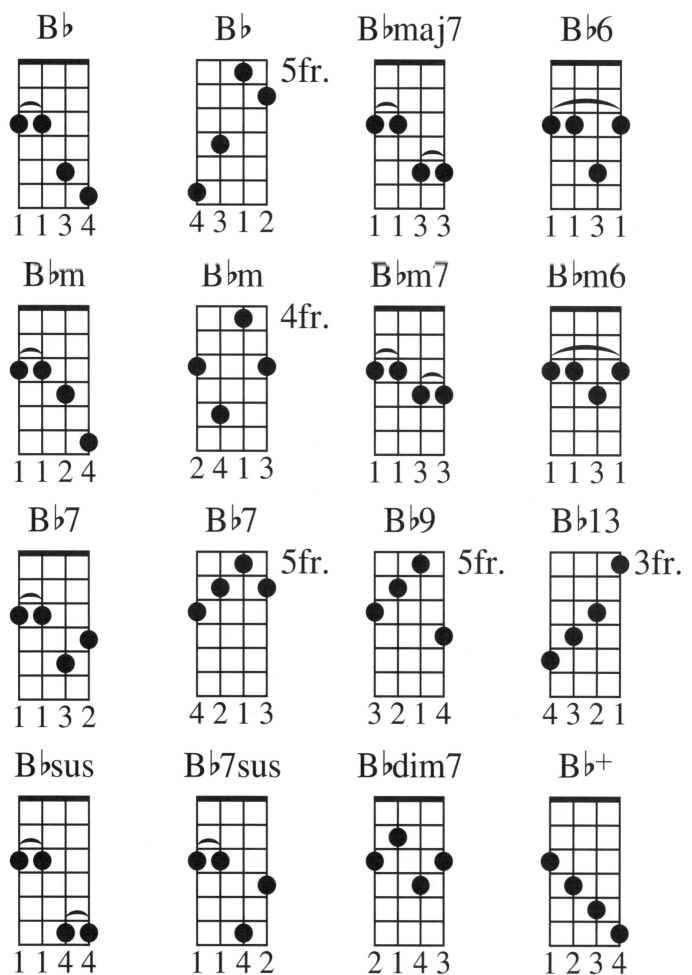

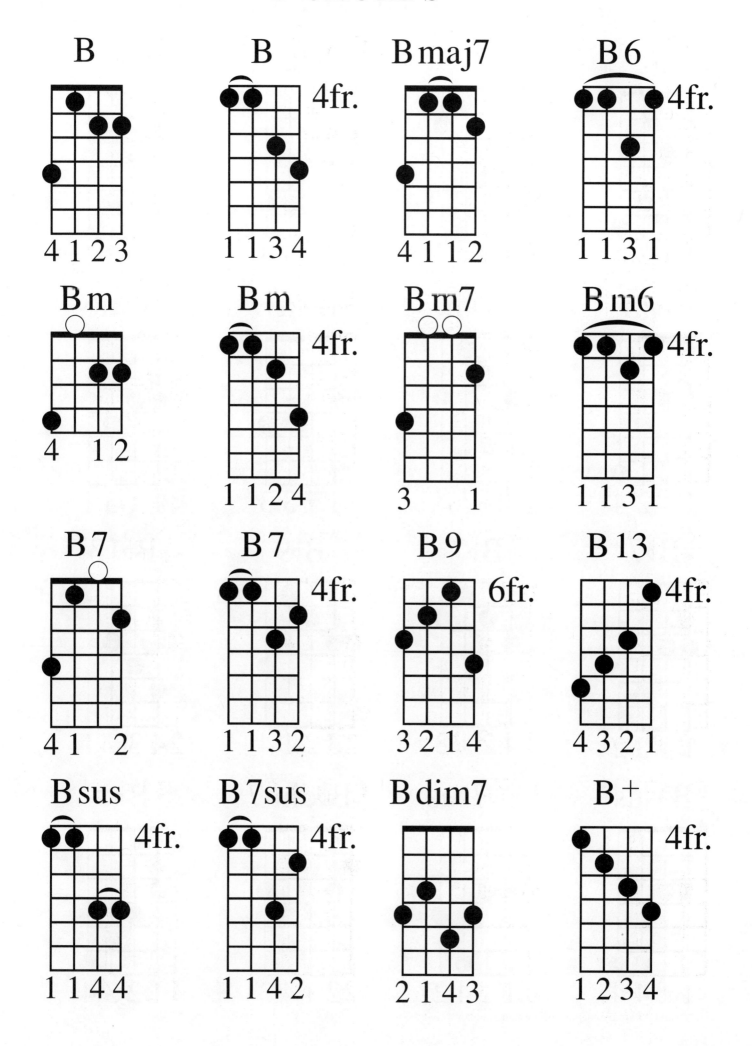

C CHORDS

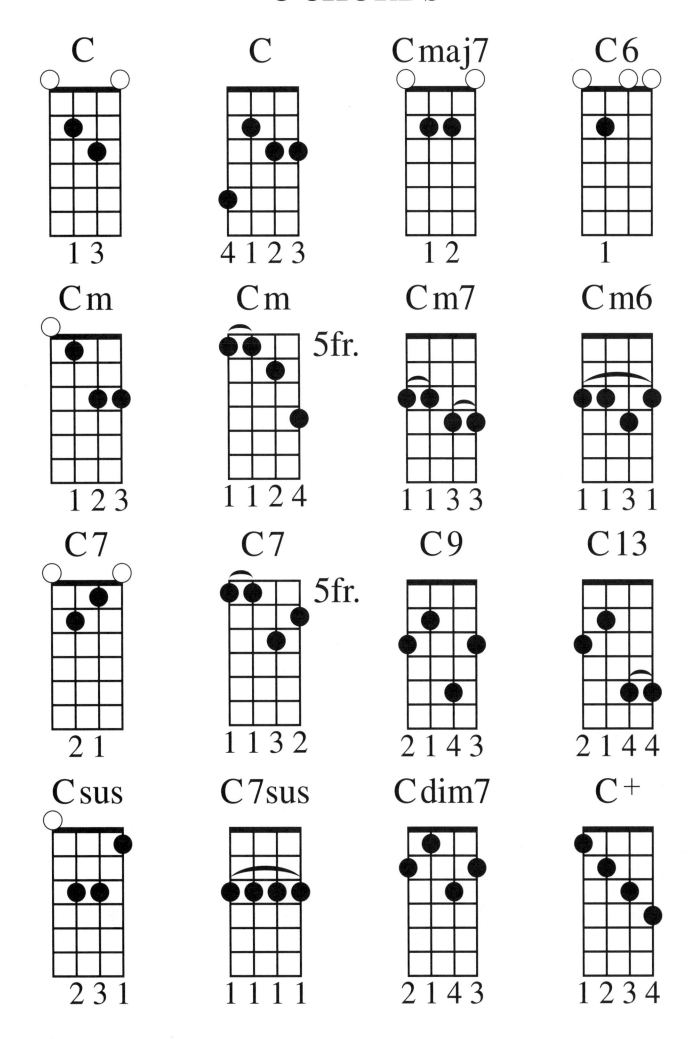

C# (Db) CHORDS*

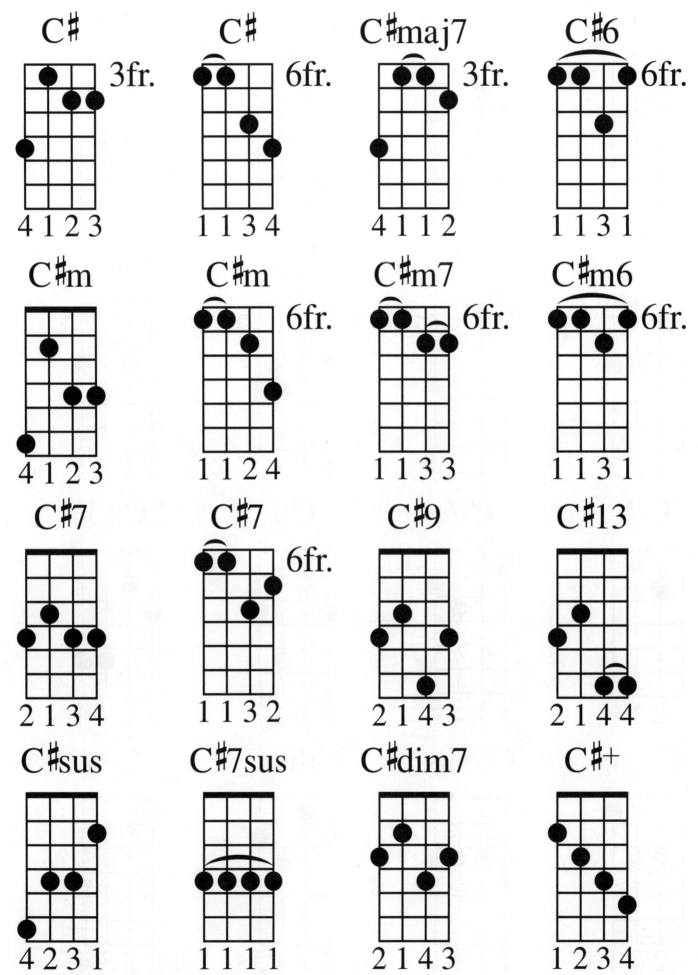

D CHORDS

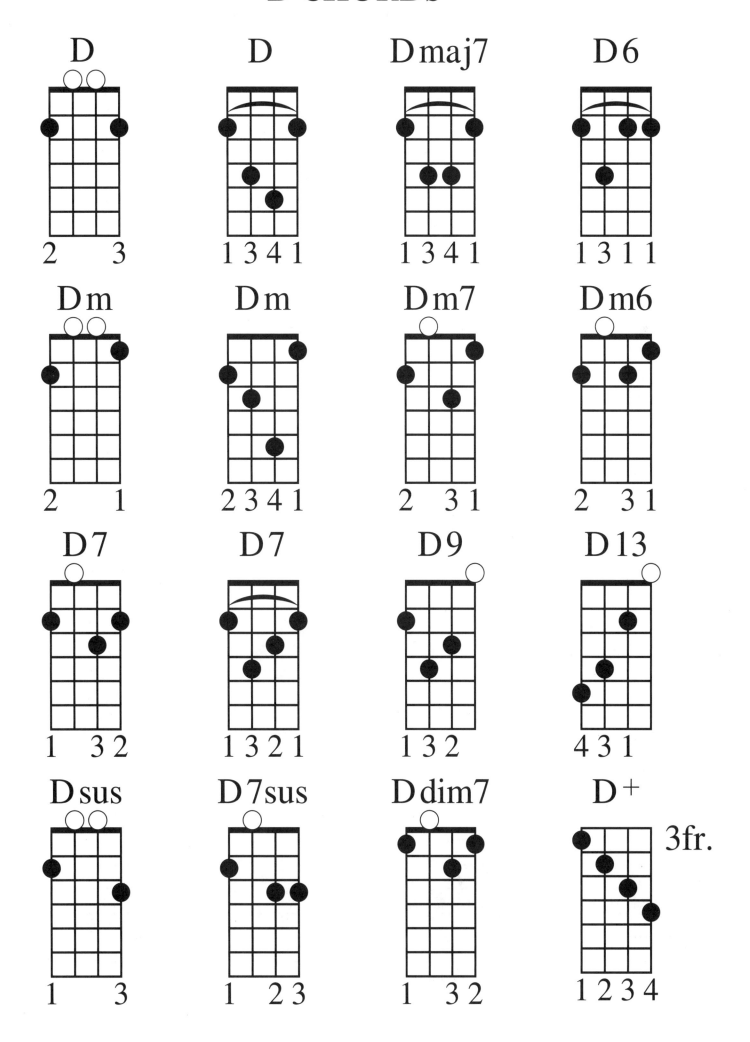

E♭ (D♯) CHORDS*

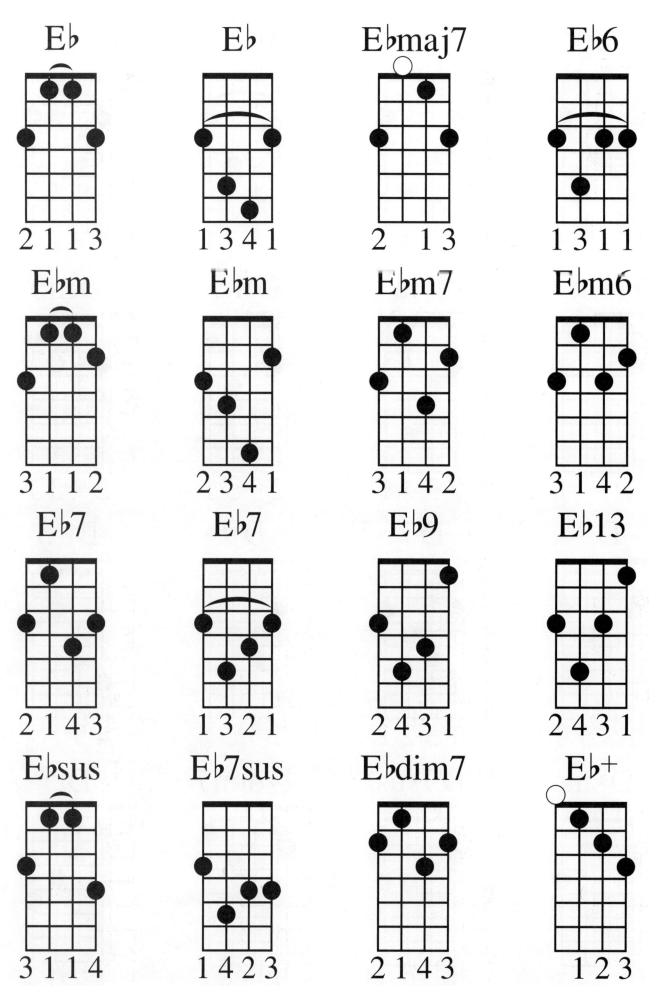

*E♭ and D♯ are two names for the same note.

E CHORDS

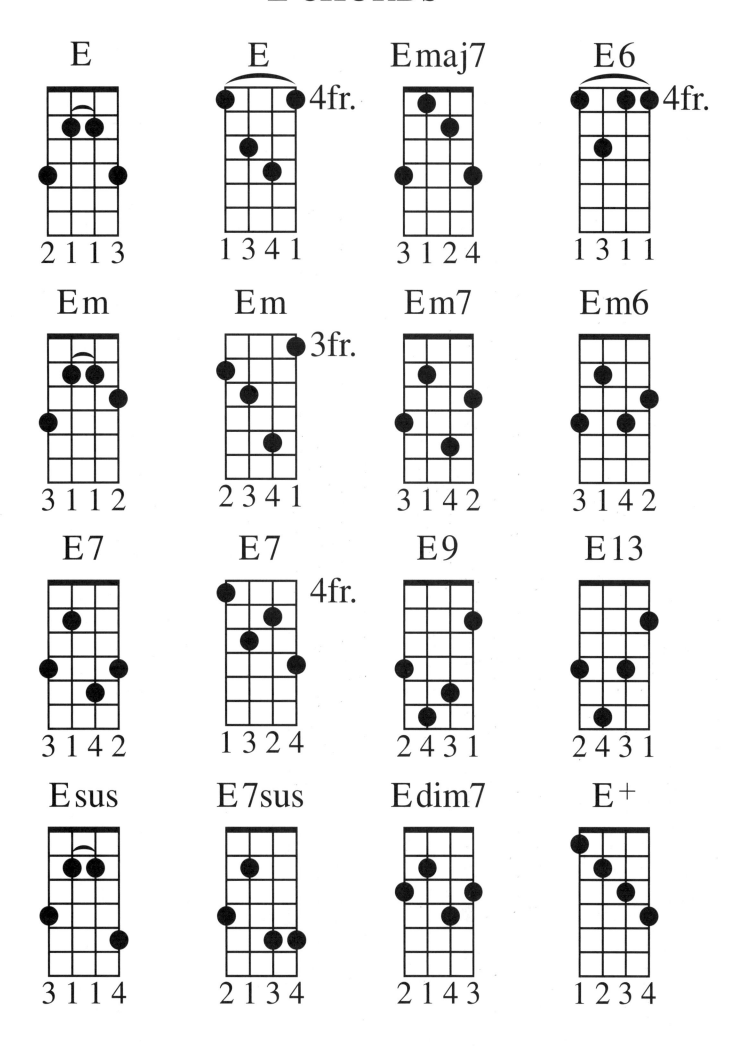

F CHORDS

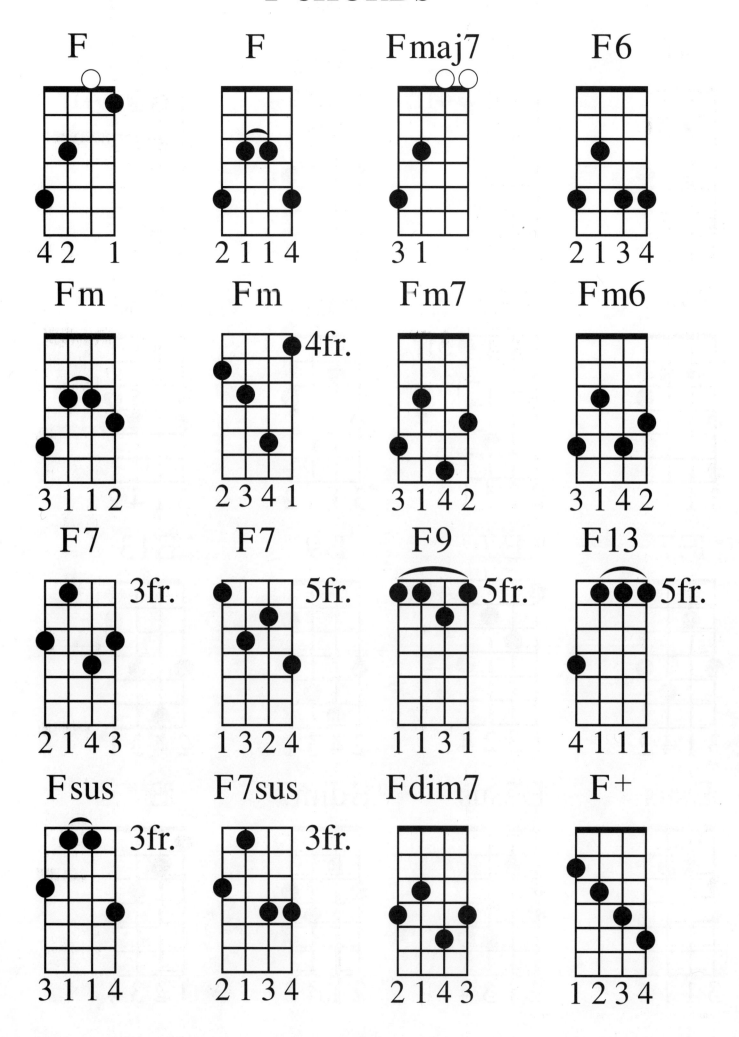

F♯ (G♭) CHORDS*

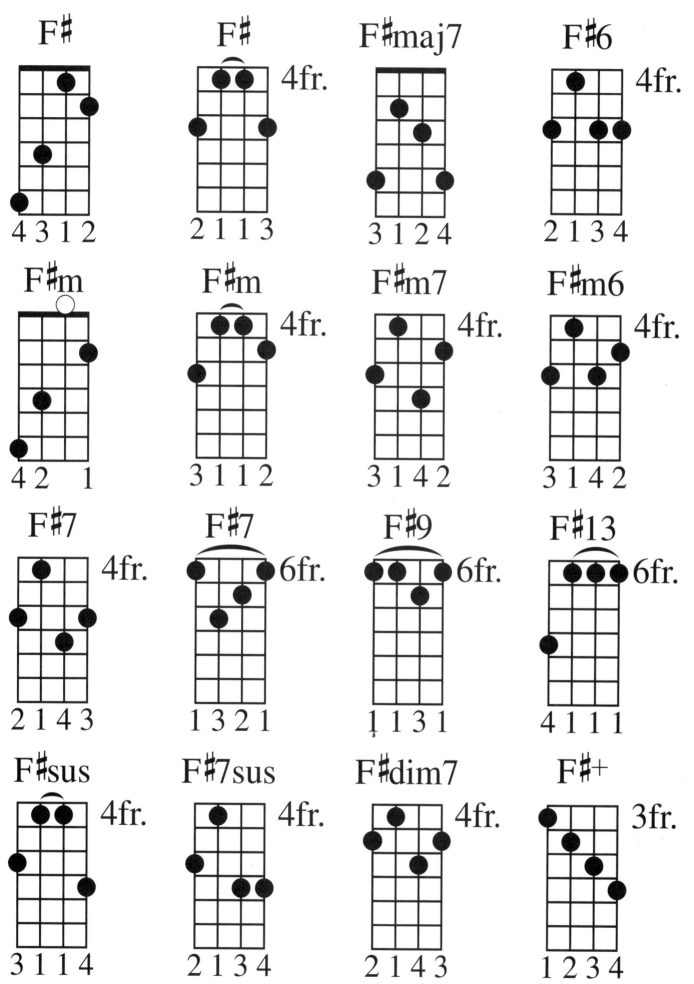

*F♯ and G♭ are two names for the same note.

G CHORDS

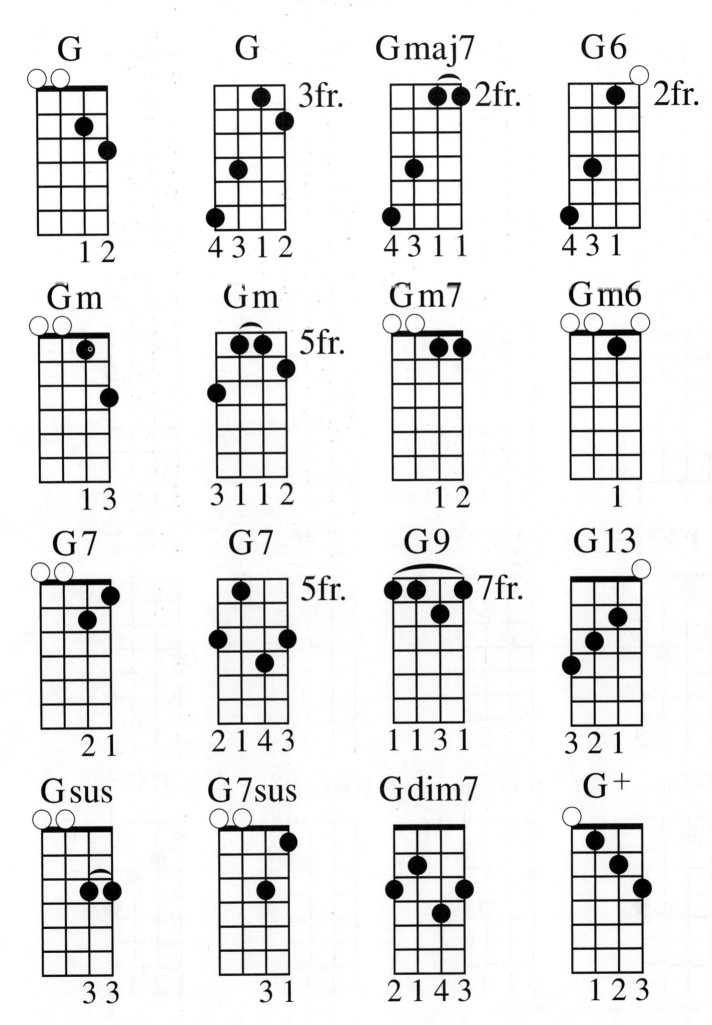

A♭ (G♯) CHORDS

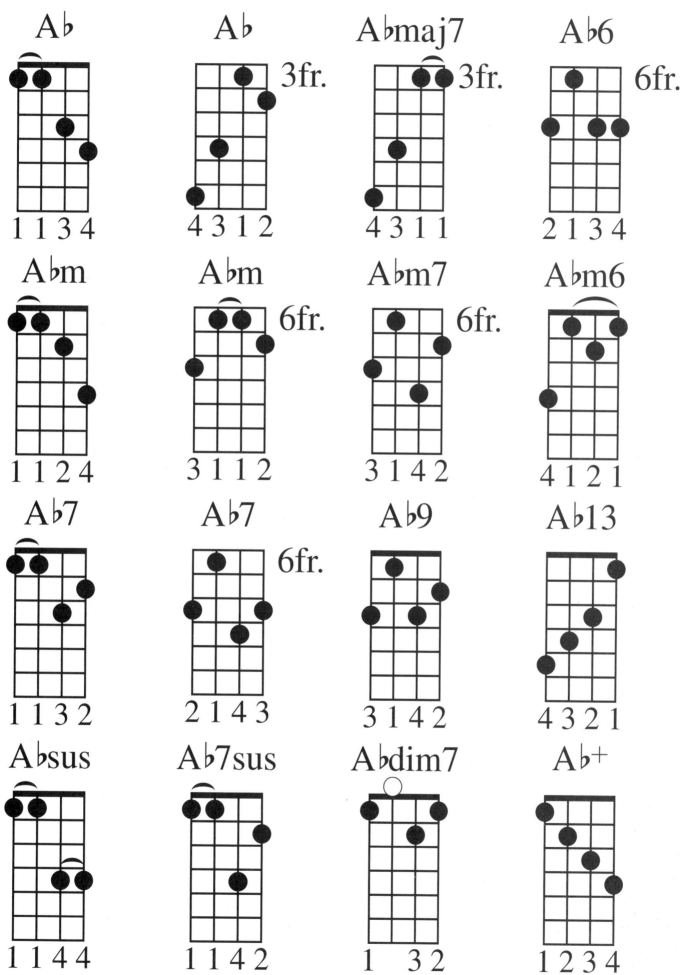

*A♭ and G♯ are two names for the same note.

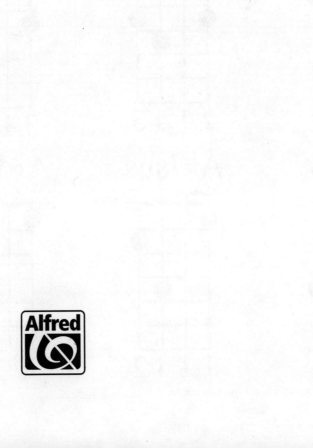